Pussy Planet

Pussy Planet

AND OTHER ENDEARING *Tales*

Kimmy Dee

MÖBIUS BOOKS

Copyright © 2016, 2019 by Kimmy Dee. All rights reserved. No part of this book may be used or reproduced in any manner whatsoever without written permission except in the case of brief quotations embodied in critical articles and reviews. For information please visit www.mobiusbooks.com.

Cover Illustrations © 2019, Chris Enterline

First printing: July 2016, Kimmy Dee
Second printing: September 2019, Möbius Books

ISBN: 978-1-7333225-0-8
ebook ISBN: 978-1-7333225-1-5

Dedicated to Jack – the funniest fucker of mothers I've ever known.

1957 -2003

CONTENTS

Pussy Planet	9
The Turd Behind the Curtain	11
Caucasian Chameleon	23
Welcome to Adulthood: There's an Ointment for That	29
It's the Thought that Sucks	43
Lame Brain	49
Domesticated Douchebags	55
A Crock of Meconium	59
Breast is… Meh, at Best	67
Same Shit, Different Shoes	73
Poppin' Bones	81
Speed Freak	83
Ovarian Horror Story	97
Ugly Fuckling	105
Losing Jack	115
Finding Pat	159
Anti-Climax	183

Pussy Planet

I'M TUCKING MY EIGHT year old daughter into bed, that age-old purgatorial chore, when her big brown doe eyes turn up to mine and she stutters a confession.

"Mommy, I accidentally said a bad word today." Her voice is timid and she's blinking back tears. "But I didn't know it was bad."

Sometimes this kid is too sweet for me. I sigh with boredom as I wait for her to continue. Was she playing a rhyming game, and inadvertently spit out a "bitch", "shit", or "fuck"? Well, everyone has to learn somehow, right? I just needed to know which word she had mistakenly said, so I could teach her to use it in the right context. Parental responsibility, and all that shit.

"What did you say?" I ask as I prepare my potential responses.

"Pussy."

I choke a little.

"Pussy?"

"Yes. Pussy." Her squeaky voice crackles with shame.

"So… what exactly did you say?" I'm going to need context for this one. The parenting blogs I occasionally peruse have never mentioned vagina slang, which is probably why they never held my interest.

"I called Bobby a pussy ball, and he said it was a bad word."

I can't help myself; I laugh. I'm aware that as a parent I'm not supposed to react, but this is too good. And I've never claimed to be a great parent.

"Why did you call him a pussy ball?" I finally manage to ask between snorts.

"Because he was angry and reminded me of a cat."

Okay, I say to myself. I can work with this. There's no need to give a whole anatomy lesson over it.

"Well," I say, "It isn't really a bad word. But you shouldn't call anyone a pussy, because it can be taken to mean that you are calling them weak."

She considers this for a moment. I see her working it over in her sweet, innocent little brain.

"In that case," she says, "there should be a pussy planet, and all boys should go live there."

I fall over laughing.

She laughs too. She doesn't even understand why it's funny, but because her mom is cackling like a lunatic she knows she just spit out some comedy gold. And that makes me laugh harder.

Eventually the laughter wears down; our cheeks hurt, our sides are cramped, but damn it feels good.

"Okay," I say, "It's time to go to sleep." I pull her covers up to her chin and kiss her on the forehead as I tiptoe to the doorway. She never lets me leave peacefully; there's always something else to say.

"But I'm afraid to sleep, because last night I had a bad dream," she says.

I pause to scan my mommy brain bank for the perfect words of encouragement to send my little angel off to sleep. Like any good mom, I just want her to go the fuck to sleep so I can kick off my nightly routine of eating chocolate and scratching my ass.

"Hey," I finally say, flipping the light switch. "Just… don't be such a pussy."

The Turd Behind the Curtain

IT'S A GLAMOROUS GIG AND ALL, but I don't recall ever answering the age-old question of 'What do you want to be when you grow up?' with 'Some douchebag that posts dick and fart jokes on the internet.' And not just because the internet didn't exist back then, although that did probably hinder any prepubescent premonitions about my future. No, in my youth I had loftier goals than reigning over a sliver of cyberspace named after a gargantuan pile of poop; I suppose we all start out a bit rosy eyed before reality kicks us around a bit. All that truly matters is that we never stop trying to delude ourselves into believing we're exactly where we want to be, or at least heading in that general direction.

  The first occupation I remember wanting to waste the rest of my life on was a labor union lawyer, which I can chalk up to my factory-employed father brainwashing me into believing I could make a living by arguing all day. And while a skilled rebutter may be able to do just that, my go-to strategy during any and all verbal disputes are "Yo Mama" jokes, and I don't think I'd win any big cases by proclaiming that opposing counsel's mama is so fat and dumb that when the judge says

"Order in the court!" she asks for fries and a shake. Plus, I eventually found out how much schooling is required to become a lawyer, and at eight years old I already knew I wasn't willing to put that level of effort into my life.

Something I did deem worthy of a little exertion, though, was faking nightmares when I heard my dad get home after working second shift so I could lay on the loveseat in the living room and pretend to sleep off my night terrors while actually watching Johnny Carson with the old man through squinted lids. This is also how I managed to see my very first horror movie at four years old, when my dad decided to skip the Tonight Show and pop in a VHS of Nightmare on Elm Street 2. I spent the next two years afraid that Freddy Krueger was going to claw his way out of my dad's chest cavity every time he kissed me good night, but what 80's kid didn't? It was a terrifying time for everyone.

But Johnny Carson exposed my fragile young mind to more than just animal hijinks. He opened my eyes to a whole new profession that was never even mentioned during kindergarten career day: the stand-up comic.

I didn't know if I had what it took to be a teacher, a nurse, a veterinarian, or any of those other bullshit professions parents tell their kids they should aspire to, but I did know I could scream my fucking face off on par with Sam Kinison, my first celebrity role model. I practiced all the time, which I'm sure made my parents incredibly proud. "Oh, your Timmy can recite fifteen hundred Bible verses? Well, my Kimmy can do the entire 'Jesus didn't have a wife' bit without missing a single guttural howl."

Plus, I had always been able to get the laugh. I was the class clown and resident playground smart-ass of my elementary school. While my quick wit and cunning delivery often got me in trouble with my teachers, I quickly earned the unwavering respect of my peers, who mostly still relied on armpit farts and the shock value of naughty words to establish their wisecracking proficiency. While my cynical disposition didn't win me a whole lot of close friends, no one really fucked with me, either. I don't think anyone wanted to risk becoming the target of my acidic tongue, and I was perfectly content with that. Admiration is admiration, after all, even when forged out of fear.

But as they do for most children, my ambitions changed when I entered the inevitable awkward period of adolescence. While still every bit the sarcastic smartass, I no longer craved attention. I still wanted to be admired and all, but I couldn't stand to have people look at me. I became obsessively self-conscious. I was sure I always looked and sounded completely ridiculous; that the very sight of me is what had people laughing, not my clever wordplay. I knew every single time someone so much as glanced in my general direction they saw me for the obnoxious troll that I truly was. The problem was my mouth still tended to spit out its scathing retorts before my agitated brain could shut it down. This led to more attention that I didn't want, and therefore, more anxiety. My life turned into a vicious one person circle jerk of suck.

Luckily it was around this time that technology came through for us attention-whoring introverts with the emergence of bulletin board systems, the precursor of social networking and first caterer to the ever-growing socially anxious geek market.

With all the glitz and glamour of a dial-up modem and a green screen computer, I was able to connect to a local BBS and fulfill my need for social interaction without having to show my face. There were no profile pictures back then, just a few lines in which a user could describe themselves, which I filled with a rotating array of angsty song lyrics. It was perfect. I was able to get the LOLs and even a few ROFLs (the precursor to LMAOs) without feeling like they were directed at my over-plucked eyebrows or ever-thickening mustache. I even made a handful of my lifelong friends through my nerdy junior high BBS habit, although I still do my best to never see them in person.

Kimmy Dee

Eventually Windows and America Online came along and shit all over everything, much like Twitter would do to the social networking scene a few years later, but by then I was in high school and had discovered drugs so I didn't really care that much. I had found with the right amount of pot and heaping helpings of disdain I could keep the crippling anxiety to a much more manageable, only slightly debilitating level. My sardonic worldview evolved into more of a full-blown hatred for everyone and everything, which was pretty much the prevailing fashion of the '90s anyway. We didn't have Grumpy Cat; we had grunge and goth. I managed to incorporate the best of both styles into my daily garb simply by tying twelve black flannel shirts around my waist and scowling all the time.

It was during that period of black lipstick-clad innocence that I decided to give writing a shot. I wrote my first short story as an assignment for my ninth grade English class, and the teacher wrote on the grading rubric that I should consider trying to get it published. That seemed much too high-reaching for the apathetic aspirations of my pubescent period, but I tucked that little nugget of praise in the back of my mind, where it slowly ate a hole through the very fabric of my soul.

Obviously that last part isn't true. I had actually lost my soul, as well as that of my first born, a decade before the pre-damned child was even conceived in a high stakes poker game. It was "high stakes" because we didn't have any actual money, so we made a running tab of items that we owed each other. You see, the first thing about economics that American kids are taught is that it doesn't matter if you can pay; that's what the next generation (and China) are for. So while I may have laid an invisible appendage of my future child on the line over a pair of deuces, I *do* hold an I.O.U. proclaiming me the rightful owner of a clump of Nicholas Cage's pubes, which I'm sure we can all agree makes me the winner.

Anyway, the unexpected compliment from my English teacher did stir up the faintest feeling of excitement, which I quickly tried to extinguish with an overdose of death metal.

The Turd Behind the Curtain

Despite the resulting tinnitus, it was still alive... a persistent parasite that has been proven fatal in every single case to the coveted grunge-goth lifestyle: the apathy-destroying desire to actually accomplish something in life.

For a few years I was able to drown that nagging little twinge of ambition in bong water and the Earth-stomping angst that only a white girl from the suburbs can muster, but every now and then it crept back into my brain that maybe, just maybe, I should dare to put some effort into something other than catching a buzz.

It was around this time in my life that my sense of humor became more of a liability than an asset. I mean, aside from the ever hilarious high-casualty natural disaster, nothing is supposed to make a grunge-goth kid smile. Kurt Cobain was dead and our parents drove minivans – life was nothing but an endless series of disappointments. And on the goth side of the spiritlessness spectrum, well, smiling in that makeup would make one hardly distinguishable from a Juggalo, and that's just plain unforgiveable. While I never did learn to control my classroom outbursts, I did at least master spewing my cynicism straight-faced. But there was still no doubt that my buffoonery hurt my street cred, which was already at enough of a dis-advantage because of that whole "white girl in the suburbs" thing.

So when it came to writing, it never even occurred to me to try to inflict humor into my embarrassingly ambitious hobby. I was trying to distance myself from that whole class clown thing. I was an artist, damn it. I was to be taken seriously.

Besides, my jokes were never thought out ahead of time, like my brilliant future novels would be. All of my quips were based on topical humor, or from run of the mill banter. It seemed that the only outlet for such tomfoolery was standup comedy, which involved that whole people looking at you thing, which had been taken off the table a few years earlier with the development of my "oh my god everyone is laughing at my eyebrows" anxiety. (For the record, my eyebrows were goddamn ridiculous from 7th grade until I finally discovered waxing in my 30s, so my fear was well grounded.)

    I wrote my first unassigned short story as a junior in high school. It was the most 90s piece of angsty drivel ever written by someone who wasn't Alanis Morissette. My intention was to keep my masterpiece of melodrama to myself, but shortly after penning its gloomy conclusion I stumbled across an ad on my school library's wall for a writing contest sponsored by the local community college. Submissions were accepted by mail-entry and required no one from my school to know that I was participating, so I figured why the hell not? If it didn't blemish my all-important blasé resume, what was the harm in testing the literary waters? I mailed off the story, chugged a little Boones Farm, and resumed my brooding as usual.

    While prepping for my senior year, I was faced with a dilemma regarding my indifference. We got to pick our poison, so to say, when it came to which English course to take in twelfth grade: College English; a class customized for those planning to do something more than meet the minimum requirements in their lives, or English 12; the remedial course, designed to at least award a diploma to those of us with just enough determination to not drop out. There was no in-between; you've heard the phrase "Go big or go home"? It was more like "Go big or go scrub toilets for the rest of your life, you worthless shit." And, in what would become a recurring theme for me in life, I chose the toilets.

    My passivity paid off, and at the beginning of my senior year I was voted the female recipient of the highly coveted "Class Slacker" award. I can only imagine the immense pride coursing through my parents' veins when their silly salutatorian-spawning friends spoke in jest of the honor bestowed upon me. So, you can imagine my surprise when, as I was probably huffing glue and coloring a picture during an otherwise regular session of English 12, my teacher asked for the class's attention so he could make an "exciting" announcement.

The Turd Behind the Curtain

While such a request was normally met with groans and spit balls, on this day the class actually piped down and let the man talk… a phenomenon that can only be explained by the existence of a higher power; an almighty ruler presiding over the entire universe, who just so happens to hate my fucking guts.

The English teacher, visibly disturbed by the sudden interest shown to him from this group of unruly miscreants, announced that he'd like to read a letter the school had received from the community college aloud. After the first few lines were read I was too busy mumbling the infamous "make me a bird" prayer from Forrest Gump to be able to recall the exact verbiage, but there was something about an area-wide writing contest that a student from our class had entered into, under their own free will.

Because they *wanted* to.

God didn't turn me into a bird that day. Instead He embarrassed the living shit out of me by awarding my stupid story second place in the writing contest and sending the notification (as well as a check for a hundred bucks, to compensate for the defamation of character that the unnecessary recognition caused) to my school instead of to my home.

Besides sullying my reputation as a sluggard, the award for my juvenile gibberish also solidified my notion that I had words waiting in my head that the world would truly want to read. I was going to be a writer! I would never have to show my stupid face, yet people would still know my name. My new career choice offered all the name recognition of stand-up comedy, with the anonymity I needed to cater to my flourishing agoraphobia.

And it was with that realization that everything went to shit.

I've been an avid reader all my life. I went from binge-reading Sweet Valley High as a kid to absorbing entire Stephen King epics as a tween, maybe with a couple of classics thrown in for good measure. By high school my literary diet consisted of nothing but death, drugs, and despair; you know, typical '90s shit. I guess I just assumed I should be writing the types of stories that I liked to read. I knew my first bestselling novel would pop into my head at any moment, and I'd be ready for the fame and fortune that was there for the taking.

Flash forward to fifteen years later... and I'm still waiting.

While I can freely admit that I was a complete dipshit for never even considering making comedy my main focus in writing, there also wasn't much of a market for it then. My "gift", if I ever really had one, was the mostly useless (at least in the pre-internet age) genre of smart-assed topical humor. I was going to write bestseller fiction, not bathroom stall one liners.

I had no desire to write humor; I already lived it. And the living wasn't all that good.

I went through many depressive episodes as a teenager. Who didn't, though? Melancholy and self-loathing are as much rites of passage as getting one's first period, or doling out that first toothy blow job. They aren't pretty, but they're necessary.

[Side note: I'm not saying doling out blow jobs is an obligatory part of graduating to womanhood; just that if you're going to, using teeth the first time is a MUST. Drive them wild, but make them fear you -- that's my teenage dating philosophy. I'm available to speak at school assemblies or church youth groups upon request.]

Unfortunately, my little "episodes" didn't improve upon reaching adulthood, and by my mid-20s I had recorded diagnoses of panic disorder and bipolar disorder, as well as a short stint as a resident in a mental health facility. While these things certainly put a damper on the wildly successful writing career I had aspired to before reality kicked me in the cunt a few times, my sense of humor hadn't suffered much. But I did shelve any literary delusions I was clinging to and focused instead on just surviving, and laughing at the absurdity of such an existence.

By my mid to late twenties, a decade into the 2000s, the world had finally gotten its shit together a little and adapted to better accommodate those of us who crave the attention and approval of others yet loathe putting on pants or leaving the house. I'm talking, of course, about the rise of the modern social network. Updating a status was so much less painful than picking up the phone, or, God forbid, going to a social gathering. I only wished I could work or wipe my kid's ass via Myspace or Facebook. We'll get there someday; I'm sure of it. Well, Myspace won't. Sorry, Tom.

But with social networking, my comedy finally found the market it needed. I worked best in small doses and without being seen, so the character limits and anonymity of online shitposting allowed me to throw caution to the breaking wind without any brain-wrenching repercussions. And my friends and family were able to hit "like" to humor me, without even having to feign a smile and then run to my mother to ask if I was properly medicated. It was a win for everyone. It may not have been a career, but I was able to make people laugh again, and that was all I really wanted. Or so I thought.

I got married for the second time in 2011, and we kept the ceremony small, but since it was my husband-to-be's first wedding (fucking overachiever) he wanted the big party, so we compromised and threw a big reception a couple of days later. I suggested that we write our own vows and read them to each other at the party, because I'm obviously a masochist when it comes to my anxiety disorder, and I thought it would be nice for the hundred or so people we had shunned with invites to the actual wedding to at least get to feel awkward while we publicly proclaimed our stupid love for each other.

I wrote my vows the day before the party in a hungover haze. I wanted to make sure to thank everyone that had helped out with both the ceremony and the reception, but also threw in a few jabs at them to keep things interesting. I scribbled in a few lines about loving my darling husband at the end as an afterthought, but the delivery made my wedding vows come off as a five minute comedic roast of my nearest and dearest friends and family. And the guests fucking loved it.

While my new husband stood there dumbfounded (and probably wishing he hadn't let me go first), I received the wedding reception version of a standing ovation. That is, people reluctantly put their free drinks down to clap with both hands. But afterwards I lost count of the amount of people that commented on my speech, and suggested I try my hand at stand-up comedy. While that's not the normal reaction one elicits from their wedding vows, I was positively glowing from the praise. Well, from the praise as well as the champagne. And the rum. And probably a few beers. But mostly the praise.

Whatever it was, it reignited that same spark my high school teacher had lit when she suggested that I try to publish my work. It made me want to write. But this time, over a decade later, I realized that humor was an integral part of me, and I had to use it.

Shortly after the wedding I started a blog called Turd Mountain, and within a few months of spouting profanities about everything from Mothers' Day to the idiocies of pop culture, while crapping out countless alliterative poop puns in every post, my social media following grew beyond just the friends and family who were obligated to love me to over ten thousand fans.

In between larger writing projects and epic mental breakdowns, I continued to spew forth filthy one liners to keep my newfound fans entertained. I began to embrace the official art of the 21st century: the meme. For the first time in my life, from safely behind the screen of my laptop, my creativity began to flow freely… albeit, mostly in the form of poop jokes. But it was enough to distract from the mundane repetitiveness of everyday life without sending my anxiety spiraling.

I took on a couple of additional writing-for-the-web gigs, getting my first big "break" when the humor giant Cracked.com published one of my articles. I went from a few hundred views on a blog post to having my name slapped on a piece that reached over a million hits in its first week. The comment section was full of adoring fans and angry trolls, the latter of which bragged about the precarious sexual positions they had just engaged in with my mother. I had achieved internet stardom.

I wrote another article for Cracked, and took on a regular role contributing to a local satire website. I did guest blog posts at a few places, including a couple of "funny mommy" sites. I was recruited to write reviews for the macabre fan site Horror-Homework.com, where it was soon determined that my reviews were boring as shit if I didn't absolutely hate the subject of my work, so I was given a regular column where I reviewed the most godawful movies ever made, aptly dubbed *Kimmy Karnage's Turds of Terror*. At two years, it was my longest running gig.

My first foray into fiction, a short story titled "Dolls of Disaster", was published in an e-book anthology appropriately titled *Crappy Shorts: Deuces Wild*. The collection was mostly a flop, but the three people that read it were kind enough to my contribution in their reviews that I've continued to play around with creating stories.

I also went through long silent periods, where dealing with my mind and daily life drained me of my desire to entertain. I often unpublished my blog and my Facebook page as I rode out the storms. But I'd always come back swinging, and since the majority of my audience did not know me on a personal level, I began to view them as another much-needed support system. When they were happy, when they were laughing, I felt better.

While most of my posts were topical, it turned out that poking fun at the very brain that plagued me so much made for some of my most popular posts. It seems many people can relate, and actually benefit from, a humorous look at what havoc a defective mind can reap. Because laughter makes enduring it all seem worthwhile, and it's good to know you're not alone.

I could never stand up in front of a room of people and tell jokes. I can't stand up in a room full of people, period. I'm a couple of cats and a disability pension away from being a complete shut in, but I'm not dead. I still want to entertain. I want to make people laugh. And I want to do it all from behind the safety of a computer screen, where no one is looking at me.

I'll never be a stand-up comic. And I'm pretty sure I'll never write a novel that goes down in history as a masterpiece of modern literature. But I do have stories to tell, and I'll do my best to make you laugh.

So please, enjoy my stories. Laugh at my jokes. All I ask from you, dear reader, is please… pay no attention to the turd behind the curtain.

Caucasian Chameleon

FOR AS LONG AS I CAN REMEMBER nearly every new person I meet – be it a schoolmate, a coworker, or a random asshole on the street – has asked me the same stupid question: "What nationality are you?"

I thought the invasive (and mildly offensive) question was just a quirk of my rural, whiter-than-rice hometown, where my black hair and olive skin seemed "exotic". When I was in first grade we were being taught about Martin Luther King, Jr., probably our alabaster class's first exposure to the reality of racism in our nation's history, and after the lesson the teacher asked if anyone had any questions. We were all sitting cross-legged on the story time carpet, our young, privileged jaws hanging open, and finally a brave young boy raised his hand.

"Yes, Geoffrey?" the teacher asked. I remember absolutely nothing of my late teens and very little of my 20s, but I'll never forget the fact that that boy from first grade's name was Geoffrey, with a "G".

"Is Kimmy black?" Gee-offrey asked timidly.

Twenty-two sets of young, crusty eyes fell upon me, the brains under their Dutch blonde hair whirring, wondering if a real live black person had been walking among them all along.

I shrugged.

I was six; I was still hoping to discover that I was actually a cat. I didn't know what "black" and "white" meant, let alone all of the hues in between. But from that point on, asshole strangers trying to pinpoint my nationality became an increasingly annoying game that would follow me fucking everywhere.

The thing is, I'm not exotic. I'm *all* white, and my rigid dance moves prove it. My DNA is nothing but a cocktail of Caucasianliness: Dutch, German, and Irish. My hair was naturally black before it started going prematurely gray, and my olive skin browns quickly in the sun. But despite my utter loathing for pumpkin spice anything, I am a white girl. To thwart any accusations of being the mailman's daughter (and to take the opportunity to use the word "thwart" in this book), I look exactly like my dad. I might be 5'6" and scrawny to his 6'3" and broad, but our matching ebony hair and thick mustaches are more conclusive than a Maury paternity test could ever be. And my dad got his dark features from his mom, who was nearly a purebred Irishwoman. She used to say we were "black Irish," which I believe is grandmother speak for "Fuck if I know, now eat your damn hamburger."

My only full-blooded sibling, my older sister, was born with white-blonde hair that eventually faded to light brown, with hazel eyes, and ivory skin. I was the night to her day, and if it wasn't for the identical bumps in the bridges of our noses no one ever would've suspected we were related. I'm sure she would've liked to have kept it that way. And because of that my hometown eventually grew accustomed to my "look", and most people quit asking. But after I grew up and left that diversity-challenged hellhole, the questions started again. Apparently the need to pin a cultural label to others is universal.

Caucasian Chameleon

I have been asked countless times if I am Middle Eastern, Native American, Lithuanian, Greek, Italian, Hispanic, Indian, Spanish, or Jewish. I can blend into nearly every ethnic crowd, only really looking completely out of place among the pasty towheads of my hometown. It seemed like a decent trait to have for a boringly white person, at least until 9/11.

In my daily life I remained securely wrapped in the warm blanket of white privilege, but that Caucasian cloak would be stripped from me the moment I'd enter an airport security line (as were my shoes, and dignity). I have never *not* been "randomly selected" for additional screening, and have even been pulled from the boarding line after passing through security for a re-check. The predictability of it became comical, but only because I didn't have to deal with being under such scrutiny on a day to day basis.

In fact the only times I've ever slid right through security checkpoints were upon reentering the United States from other countries, which is also funny, but in a completely terrifying way.

I turned 19 less than two weeks after 9/11, and my sister was a student at Lake Superior State University in Michigan's Upper Peninsula, just south of the Canadian border. In fact the city on each side of the bridge has the same name: Sault Ste. Marie. (That's Soo-Saint-Marie, for all of you non-Mitteners.) Since the legal drinking age in Canada is 19, a sisterly visit and Canadian bar crawl became my top priorities for ringing in my last year of teenagerdom.

At that time you didn't need a passport to enter Canada, just a birth certificate and photo I.D. The Sault (that's Canadigan slang for the town, if you're not hip to tundra talk) had actually been listed as a potential terrorist target after the 9/11 attacks, as it does contain a major international waterway, so we were stopped and questioned on our way into Canada.

It was my sister, two of her college friends, my boyfriend, and myself in the car. The customs officer examined both forms of everyone's identification, and asked several questions.

It's somewhat uncomfortable to have a customs official ask what your business in Canada is and all you have to offer is "I want to get black out drunk legally," but I'm sure underage drinking is the second most popular motive they hear, next to affordable health care.

After about fifteen tense minutes of questioning and credential checking we were allowed to pass; we had been begrudgingly welcomed into Canada.

And true to our vow, we got totally shitfaced. One of the bars we stopped at was even "raided" by Canadian police, during which our IDs were once again inspected and scrutinized. But we were legal and continued pouring booze into our heads until the bars eventually closed, and we had no choice but to head back to the home of the free.

Cue the panic.

We were drunk, other than having a vagina I fit the "potential terrorist" profile perfectly, and we were attempting to reenter the United States two weeks after terrorist attacks fucked everything up forever. And did I mention we were drunk? Even our driver had a healthy buzz on, and I was certain we were headed to wherever they tortured enemies of the state prior to Gitmo. Somewhere in Indiana, probably.

In the car we all attempted to slap on our best sober faces as we pulled jerkily up to the customs station. The officer leaned in the driver's window.

"How many of ya?" He said, blinding everyone with his flashlight.

"F-f-f-five," our designated drunk driver stammered.

"All Lake State students?"

"Yup."

My stomach dropped. My boyfriend and I weren't students; as soon as he ran our IDs he'd know the driver was lying. We were fucked. Goodbye, family and friends. It's been a hell of a—

"Go on through." The officer motioned us on, and headed to the next car. He didn't even ask for our IDs.

Seriously?

Caucasian Chameleon

We were waved back into post-terror America as though we were parking at a county fair, and while I was thrilled to not be detained by customs police, the passivity of the border patrol didn't give me any warm fuzzies about our nation's security. But at least I was able to puke into a star-spangled toilet that night. God bless America.

***

I had a similar experience when I traveled to Jamaica in 2004 on my first honeymoon. I was thoroughly searched, questioned, poked, and prodded before being allowed to leave the United States, but upon my reentry I was simply asked how much booze I had brought back with me and then sent on my Yankee Doodle way.

But despite my reptilian ability to adapt to any ethnic environment, outside of airports I've always reaped the bullshit benefits that come free with being a white girl.

In my late teens I worked second shift in a dodgy area of town. I was frequently pulled over on my way home, but rarely cited; presumably the stops were just to see if I would pass the officer's intuitive sobriety test. I lived near a coworker and friend, Jason, who happened to be a black man that drove a low riding Caddy. If we left work at exactly the same time, driving the same roads, he was always the one to be stopped. And he was rarely let go with a bullshit story about a stolen car matching the description of his, and an apology for his troubles. Instead he was given tickets for going 3 mph over the speed limit, or for misadjusted headlamps. The tickets might as well have listed "being black after midnight" as the offense.

While it's all fun and games for me to play "what orifice of mine will the TSA search this time!" whenever I enter an airport, what I've dealt with is only scratching the surface of the discrimination that true non-whites face on a daily basis.

I've started answering the "What are you?" question with whatever I feel the asker wants to hear. Most of my coworkers now think I'm from Mumbai, despite my nasally Midwestern accent. Because, honestly, if you need to know what nationality I originate from in order to calculate how you should judge me, you've already made up your mind. Plus it makes me seem way more edgy when I tell white jokes, and I need all the help I can get.

If you really are just dying to know how white someone is, throw on some Springsteen and see how rigidly they dance. Despite having a booty even J. Lo would be jealous of, my hips have all the rhythm of an arthritic hippopotamus with a branch jammed up its ass. And even though my dark complexion has rendered me immune to the aromatic allure of Bath & Body Works lotion, don't ever try to throw down your yoga mat in front of mine. Because seriously, I like literally can't even.

Welcome to Adulthood: There's an Ointment for That

EVERYONE HAS DIFFERENT NOTIONS about what it takes to become an adult. A mental checklist, if you will, of the rites of passage one must pass through in order to shed the cocoon of adolescence; to finally unfurl the wings of maturity, with all the inherited wisdom and coaching from the carefree days of youth culminating in that breathtaking moment where the once timid kid emerges from the chrysalis of childhood, taking flight as a confident and independent adult ready to take their rightful place in the world. To some, this metamorphosis occurs magically at age 18. To others, after graduating from high school or college. I'm sure a few hold out for that special moment when the ungrateful little parasite finally gets a real job and moves himself and those goddamn video games he's so fond of out of the basement, so we can maybe build that rec room we've always wanted before we fucking die.

As for my own passage into post-pubescence, well, I blossomed into a full-blooded adult with all the fanfare one might expect to be bestowed upon an intelligent, creative young woman with the whole world at her fingertips: a skipped graduation ceremony, a drowned car, and an itchy crotch.

It wasn't even the real graduation ceremony that I bailed on. I went to public school in a town where at least 90% of the public were towheaded Bible thumpers, so they held a separate commemoration before the actual diploma-receiving debacle, in which everyone would hold hands and pray that the newly liberated youths would lead Godly lives. (Apparently that means always turning away from the temptation of sin, which typically takes the form of a mysterious hole in a rest stop bathroom stall, and cramming Christ down the emaciated throats of starving children on church-sponsored mission trip vacations.)

But this spiritual circle jerk had to be held separately, as well as be optional for all students, because some uppity liberal would always cry "separation of church and state!" whenever the unarguable truth "My God is the only God; believe in him or burn in eternal hellfire" was mentioned in a state-funded schoolhouse.

Despite being born there, I was already an anomaly because of my hair and skin tone. Once the whole "excommunicated Catholic, disinterested Protestant" religious status was thrown in, it was clear that I did not belong in that town. But my mother and stepfather were respected citizens in the community, and my four older siblings had begrudgingly participated in the baccalaureate ceremony, as one final dogmatic display to appease the parental units. But I could not stomach another sacrificed afternoon of pretend prayer, especially with my jerkoff classmates.

Getting out of it wouldn't be easy, though. I remembered two years earlier when my sister refused the same service. Many weeks of arguing, demanding, and door slamming passed, and then, on that dreaded Sabbath, my sister donned her Sunday best and sang *Kumbaya* with her classmates. I know this because I was bitterly mumbling along in the bleachers with the rest of my family.

I spent a greater portion of my senior year plotting how to get out of the prayer party than I did studying, which isn't saying much. But that realization became my out. My sister, despite her pending legal adulthood status, still needed to conform. She was going to college, a good portion of which our parents were paying for, and between semesters she would be returning home. I, on the other hand, didn't have that whole "life's ambition" thing counting against me, and I already had a full-time job and an apartment lined up when graduation peeked over the horizon. Sure, my mom was cosigning on the apartment since I was only seventeen, but what was she going to do, retract her signature and keep me at home? I was the final live-in dependent of five; they wanted me out. They wanted that fucking rec room in the basement.

So when I finally approached my mother with my carefully rehearsed "You cannot force me to do this" speech, I was both shocked and disappointed when she accepted my "I am not going to go to the stupid baccalaureate ceremony" with nothing but a dismayed "Fine, but I'm very disappointed."

Well, that was anticlimactic.

My mom's weak attempt at a guilt trip was the only punishment she'd attempt for my impiety, but I should have known I wouldn't be let off the hook that easily. For the Smalltown, USA God was a vengeful God, with His own set of rules and retributions.

AN EXCERPT FROM THE BOOK OF SUBURBIA, CHAPTER 4, VERSE 20:

Thou shalt erect a church on each corner; and thou shalt not giggle at the word "erect";

Thou shalt present thyself at thy chosen church each Sabbath; menfolk shall gather to discuss softball league strategy, womenfolk shalt take notice of all other women not in attendance and make a mockery of their families;

Thou shalt only buy liquor outside of town;

Thine grass must always be freshly cut, and thou shalt only cut in the earliest hours of dawn, and thine act of lawn maintenance must be loud enough to both awaken and appease the Lord;

What happens behind closed doors does not matter to the Lord, as long as thine asses and thine money hit the pew on Sunday;

Thine minivan or SUV must be adorned with a Jesus fish sticker, thereby alerting other drivers that you are above complying with any and all traffic laws;

If thine salvation has not been purchased by thy parents by way of private schooling, thou shalt invite Jesus into the heathen public school at each and every opportunity. He can't enter unless he's invited; he's like a vampire, except you drink *his* blood.

Lastly, thee must only pray when someone is watching; this shows others how superior you are to them.

Amen, and shit.

So, on the night preceding my final day of high school, with my only hurdles to freedom being four measly class periods, my mom laid down some guilt… and God threw open the floodgates.

It rained for forty days and forty nights. At least it fucking felt like it, what with my mom's continuous nagging about the fate of my eternal soul. Or maybe she just wanted me to clean my room, I don't know. I wasn't really listening. Besides, I was much more concerned about an uncomfortable itch developing in my nether region.

Vengeance was still pouring down from heaven in the morning when I hopped in my K-car and headed to the high school for the last time as a lowly student. I would have been

Welcome to Adulthood

all smiles, except that irritating itch had suddenly become a serious situation, and it was all I could do to not sit down and scoot my vagina across the floor like a dog trying to shake off a dangly turd. Still, my spirits were pretty high as I pulled out of the driveway that morning, even if I was grinding my gear against the upholstery a little harder than was absolutely necessary.

I lived on a short rural road that stretched between two equally rural roads, which essentially meant I had only two options to get out of the country mile of hell that passed for my neighborhood. I headed the direction I normally took to school, but the intersection sat at the bottom of a large hill, and had apparently transformed into a small lake during the deluge of the past twenty-four hours, complete with the octagonal fin of a stop sign stalking a windowless van that was nonchalantly bobbing along in the surf.

It was pretty obvious that my little shitmobile couldn't contend with that kind of current so I turned around and headed the other direction, still much more concerned about the state of my crotch than a bit of standing water on the roads.

I made it to an actual intersection on my second effort, and celebrated by adjusting my jeans enthusiastically. Perhaps if I had been paying less attention to my malfunctioning pussy and more to the road ahead, disaster could have been averted. But such is the fate of the sinner and the saint, and though I could have turned either left or right onto higher ground, I took control of my life and decided to charge straight ahead.

In hindsight, that was stupid. Straight ahead the road ran low, and without a floating van for perspective, I had no idea how deep the standing water actually was. At least, not until the nose of my car took a dive and the water surged over the hood, drowning the engine and turning my car into a rudderless raft, forlorn and adrift upon the sea of sorrow.

Fuck.

I rolled down the driver's window of my Dodge dinghy to assess the situation. The fenders were almost completely sub-merged. The water lapped tauntingly against my door like a cat toying with a mouse before ripping its throat out. I tried to restart the car, but it was dead. The water was too deep to open the door. I could crawl out the window, but then what? Wade through waist-deep water to no place in particular, abandoning my vehicle? It was the year 2000 and cell phone technology was in its infancy, so only executives, drug dealers, and Zack Morris had them. I was on my own.

I glanced in my rear view, and it appeared that my troubles were over. My sister, home from college for the summer, was stopped at the intersection I had crossed right before plunging straight into the swampy abyss.

I leaned out of the window and waved both arms at her, and despite the distance between us, I could feel her eyes lock onto mine. Sometimes, especially during times of distress, there exists an almost psychic connection between close siblings. You'll feel each other's pain, share in one another's sorrow. Sense when the other is in trouble. Relief washed over me and I sent a subliminal smile to my heroic older sister, who was coming to my rescue.

Then the bitch turned left.

I could see her smirk as she pulled away from the flood zone, leaving me to rot for all eternity in my watery grave. I telepathically screamed to her that she was a rat-faced whore and as soon as I got home I would literally crap all over every-thing she loves, but I'm not sure the message went through. After all, Extra Sensory Profanity Transference is not a perfect science. Hopefully we'll get there someday.

Meanwhile, in my boat-car, I was growing much more concerned about the irritation in my undies. Being set adrift with no means of returning to the mainland was unpleasant, but manageable. I had a pack of cigarettes and a bag of Skittles in the car; I'd survive. Hell, it was better than school. But a faulty vagina was beyond my capacity to deal.

No one was going to rescue me. The river on the road wasn't going to magically dry, and my vagina wasn't just going to mend itself, although I found out years later when that sucker stretched out wide enough to let a kid pass through that those things really are quite self-sufficient in the whole "maintenance and repair" department. Are you listening, car companies? Stop naming your new models after clouds and Greek gods; I'd rather drive a Labia or a Cervix any day. Especially if those dream machines were manufactured by Vulva.

I lit a cigarette to show I meant business with my newfound adulthood, and also to take my mind off my disgruntled genitals, and almost immediately flung it into the water as I saw a pickup truck approaching. It was a small town, and my mom always got pissed when I was busted for smoking.

Okay, so I wasn't all that confident in my newfound maturity just yet, but Rome wasn't built in a day.

Right after concluding that no one was going to swoop in and save me, it appeared that the stranger in the pickup truck was planning to do just that. Either that or he was going to drag me into the woods and murder me, but part of being an adult is weighing the risks against the rewards, and I figured worst-case-scenario at least I'd be out of the car and preoccupied with something bigger than pubic distress.

The pickup's wheels plodded like the Proud Mary through the flooding on the road, the driver leaning out his window as it lined up with mine, although his was a foot or two higher above sea level.

"Hi there, ya stuck?"

It took every ounce of adult in me to not say, 'Nah, just setting out on a voyage around the world in my new state-of-the-art sail-car. The middle of this road seemed like as good of a starting point as any.'

Instead, I mumbled, "Sure am."

He asked if I would like some help, and once again I swallowed my sarcasm, like any grown woman with any sense of propriety would, and managed to spit out, "Yes, please."

The pickup driver reached behind his seat and pulled out a tow strap, because what self-respecting redneck wouldn't be carrying a few of those around with him, and maneuvered the truck around until he had us hooked together. He slowly pulled me out of the water and into the muddy, vacant parking lot of the produce company that manned the fields on both sides of the low-lying road.

I made a couple more efforts to start my car with no luck, and the pickup driver asked where I was headed.

"The high school," I said. "Just down the road." As if there was any other high school within a twenty mile radius.

"Well hop in, I'll drive ya up there," he said with a smile. A fully toothed one, at that. I figured my guardian angel would be a tattooed drag queen, not a hillbilly with an orthodontist. The small town Lord works in mysterious ways.

I grabbed my backpack, cigarettes, and Skittles, and left my Dodge to rot in the dirt; my obnoxiously lifted four-wheel drive chariot awaited.

I briefly considered being embarrassed by being dropped at school by an older gent in a giant truck, but this was my last day as a student, and I didn't give a solitary fuck. Plus, my little suburbia was still a farming community at heart, and the half of the town that didn't live adjacent to a golf course slept within a stone's throw of a muck field, so the school's parking lot was a mixture of wannabe monster trucks and hand-me-down BMWs. Being neither a farmer nor a yuppie, being dropped off muddy and late in a souped-up pickup was as close as I'd ever come to fitting in. It figured that on my last day in the shithole where I was born and raised I would finally feel at home; thankfully my chafed coochie kept me from getting too comfortable.

I strategically sat upon the spiny sole of my shoe in first period, gently rocking back and forth while contemplating my most pressing predicament: what to do about my wounded clam.

I had access to a pay phone (Google it, kids) while I was at school, but who to call? Despite having one her whole life, my mom's wise teaching on the inner workings of the vagina boiled down to "Those bastards sure bleed a lot. Here, have some chocolate!" so I didn't figure it worth the quarter to call her. However, my mom had directed me to Planned Parenthood for all of my birth control needs, and they seemed pretty knowledgeable about lady flowers. At the very least they seemed to have a fascination with poking at them before doling out pills. I decided between class periods to give them a call.

Despite the Planned Parenthood receptionist's disappointment at not being able to buy any aborted fetuses from me she was very friendly, and connected me to a nurse who assured me that I was probably not dying. After talking for several minutes on a pay-phone in my crowded high school lobby about the gritty details of my ailing snatch, I wasn't so sure evading death was such a great thing. I mean, I had a healthy case of the last day fuck its and all, but I still wasn't totally keen on the idea of anyone's last impression of me including a frenzied, one-sided conversation regarding the color and consistency of my vaginal discharge. It turned out my patented indifference did have limits.

The nurse asked if I'd ever had a yeast infection before, at which point I gasped and feigned the offense I assumed one should take at such a question. I was a lady, for fuck's sake; not a goddamn bread factory.

"Since it's your first time you should probably be examined," she said. She scheduled me an appointment for after school, and I made my way to my next class, proud that I had taken the right steps to properly care for my debilitated shame cave.

That is, until I remembered I had no way to get to my appointment.

Fuck.

The rest of the school day passed languidly, made awkward not so much because of my smoldering twat, but the need to avoid all the phony, tearful "last day" drama. People were falling all over one another in the hallways, hugging and crying as if we hadn't all hated seeing each other's stupid faces every day for the past twelve years. I had to make it through the maze of manufactured camaraderie, preferably untouched, yet still sweet talk someone into giving me a ride home.

Fortune did smile on me once that day, when in the end-of-the-day melee I locked eyes with a hick that was every bit as apathetic as I was about the whole "goodbye forever" thing. He kind of shrugged at me as he adjusted his giant belt buckle, and I swooped in and asked if he could maybe give me a lift home, knowing damn well that a tried and true country boy would never leave a distressed gal stranded.

"Sure can, but we gotta go now," he said, with a southern drawl that made absolutely no sense since he had lived his entire life in Michigan.

Perfect.

Despite our different backgrounds and personalities, I had shared a classroom with this guy since preschool. We had shared so much of our lives together without ever really thinking about it. We had grown up together, went through so many of life's ups and downs. And we both knew our upcoming graduation ceremony would be the final fork in our road, as we would each take a drastically different path, our lives destined to never converge again. We both contemplated this silently as we rode the three miles between the school and my home.

He pulled into my driveway, and we both realized that this was probably it. There was no time for socializing during graduation; after I got out of that car we would probably never speak again.

"Welp, see ya," he said, shifting the car directly from drive to reverse.

"Yep, later," I returned as I hopped out of the vehicle and headed for the house. He was peeling out of the driveway before I hit the front door.

Goodbyes are hard.

I was so busy being sentimental over parting ways with good old what's-his-face that I hadn't noticed my sister's car in the driveway, but as soon as I barged into the house I was facing down my number one foe; my own flesh and blood, the deserter. She was sitting on the couch, inhaling some sort of bagged snack food, her treasonous eyes glued to the TV.

Welcome to Adulthood

I wanted to scream at her. I wanted to take all the rage that I had held in all fucking day, from the sunken car to my throbbing cunt, and hurl it all into her smug, yet unsuspecting face. I wanted to throw shit. I wanted to punch things. I also kind of wanted to fill the bathtub with lotion and sit in that bitch until my coochie quit crying. But mostly I just wanted to inflict pain on someone other than myself, and who better than my own sister? After all, she was right in front of me. And defenseless, thanks to the fine cheesy powder coating her fingertips, which she absentmindedly rubbed together over the bag, causing her manhandled snack sand to fall back into the bag before she swooped in for her next bite. I opened my mouth, ready to spew venom, when it happened: I got adulty.

"Hi," I said, in the friendliest voice I could muster. "Cool pajamas."

"Thanks," she said, glancing up briefly before returning her gaze to the TV.

"So," I said, perching myself on the arm of the couch, both to position myself near her and to sneak in a little strategic itching, "I really need your help."

I proceeded to confide all of my embarrassing problems to her: the car, the crotch, and how I was unable to get some much-needed help for the latter without the use of the former. She said she hadn't even seen me floating around in the street during her morning commute, and I pretended to believe her, because that's what adults do. There was no point bickering about it. Not when I needed something.

Because, you see, that's what being an adult is all about: degradation and manipulation.

I certainly didn't want to tell my sister about my ramshackled gash. I may talk about it freely now, but at age 17 I don't think I would have sworn under oath that I even *had* a vagina, let alone that there was something wrong with it. But humility occasionally begets pity, and any good grown up knows that from pity often comes charity. Because if you can't beat them, make them feel sorry enough for you that they'll do something to help you out to make you shut up.

Kimmy Dee

That afternoon my sister, with her dumb able-bodied vagina, drove me to Planned Parenthood. She waited in the lobby, the Mother Theresa to my wretched sex wrinkle, while at long last my feet found the stirrups for which they had been yearning.

A few pokes and prods later, the doctor's face emerged from between my stretched thighs and spoke the words I had been waiting to hear that whole agonizing, tortuous day: "It's just a yeast infection; we have an ointment for that."

Epilogue

While my love muffin found relief that very afternoon, it took a little longer to resuscitate my car. After a few failed attempts to get it started on my own, a week or so later I was out on a motorcycle ride with a friend (because I was an adult, and I'd risk splattering my brains on the side of the highway if I wanted to) and we stopped by the abandoned parking lot that I feared would become its final resting place. My friend decided he wanted to try his hand against the sodden beast.

Bill's tinkering came to no avail, but as we closed the hood and hopped back onto his Harley a stranger waltzed up and asked what the trouble might be. There were no other cars around, and the small dirt lot was situated between two fields. It was like Field of Dreams, except it didn't drag on for nearly two agonizing hours. I explained about the flooding, and he said he was mechanically inclined and would take a look at it if I wanted to leave him my keys. I used my newfound adulthood to try to rationalize the situation: this guy seemed to materialize out of nowhere, I didn't know him from Adam, and the car had become nothing more than a glorified paperweight to me by now.

After weighing the evidence, I tossed the interloper my keys. Part of being a grown-up was placing trust in complete strangers, right? Besides, what did I have to lose, other than an expensive pile of scrap metal that I probably could easily have had fixed if I'd just call a damn tow company already?

Welcome to Adulthood

Alright, maybe I didn't really think about that part, but I scribbled down my phone number, jumped on the back of the bike, and went home.

The next day the meddling drifter called. He had gotten my car running again, and would charge me only for the parts, which totaled a whopping twenty bucks. My mom drove me down to the scene of the would-be crime. I shook my hero's hand, gave him a check, started my car on the first try, and drove off toward my unfurling destiny… which was mostly comprised of more vagina adventures and a lot of cats.

To this day, that check has never been cashed. The adulthood lesson here, of course, is always trust strangers, a life philosophy that has yet to backfire, and take good care of your goop chute. After all, you might end up putting it to its God-intended use with the aforementioned strangers in a sleazy bar bathroom, because you're a goddamn adult and it's time to act like it.

And remember: if at first the itch doesn't recede, well, there's an ointment for that.

It's the Thought that Sucks

MY BELOVED SISTER'S BIRTHDAY is coming up, but I'm not buying her a damn thing. It's not because we aren't close; actually, we're quite the opposite. Of course we hated each other's guts growing up, as all good sisters are supposed to, but once Jaime went away to college she became one of my nearest and dearest friends, and remains so to this day... as long as she doesn't fucking touch me. I don't care if we are in our thirties, I don't want to catch her cooties.

So it's not a matter of a strained relationship. And it's also not because I'm cheap, although she is the doctor in the family, so if anyone's doling out presents it really should be her. But my inferiority complex is a subject for another essay, or at the very least something I should discuss with my therapist. I bet Jaime doesn't even need a therapist. That overachieving, well-adjusted whore.

It's just that, for us, the art of gift giving has been cursed. Not in some diabolical voodoo or vindictive gypsy's spell sort of way; it's more of a stupidity curse. Some half-witted hex cast by an adolescent alchemist too amused by his own farts to fully appreciate the power of the black arts. A whoopee cushion warlock, if you will.

Kimmy Dee

Anyway, I am the youngest of a Brady Bunch mutation sort of a family, minus the wholesomeness and benevolent charm. Jaime, my only "blood" sibling, is 22 months my senior. My mother always insisted our age gap is only 22 months, *not* two years, and therefore we should get along goddamnit. When Jaime graduated high school and went off to college (apparently some people do that) I was suddenly left all alone with the parental units, who had been itching for an empty nest for over two decades, and could suddenly smell their freedom.

(Their freedom, by the way, smelled a lot like pot smoke drifting up from my basement bedroom. Shhh.)

At 17 years old and the only kid left I was ready to get the fuck out of there; I couldn't wait another second to escape from the apocalyptic hell of my privileged, suburban upbringing, and my mom and stepdad were too busy high fiving and drawing up plans for their new rec room to try to stop me.

At that time my hometown was going through the normal transitional effects of urban sprawl; the old-school farm folk being invaded by the new wealthy, who were springing up housing developments and golf courses over acres upon acres of bankrupt fields. I never quite fit in, as I didn't have either an obnoxiously large belt buckle or a country club membership. Plus, aside from the migrant workers tending the few remaining celery fields, I had the darkest skin most of those assholes had ever seen. That much whiteness can be suffocating. Not to mention blinding; those bastards were *really* pale. I once had a near death experience at the local park. I had fallen asleep in the grass, and awoke to bright light all around me. Then I noticed the angels' singing sounded more like bratty ginger kids fighting over a Pogo Ball, and I realized that I hadn't died in my sleep at all -- it was just shorts season in the suburbs.

So less than a month after graduating high school I got the fuck out of that town. I rented an apartment with a flamboyant friend in a historic district of Grand Rapids, the closest excuse for a real city. ("Historic district", by the way, is just jargon in any city for "laughably outdated, dilapidated drug zone.")

It's the Thought that Sucks

This place was so shitty that there were monthly "bulletins" posted in the apartment building's lobby recapping the recent crimes in the area. Most were theft and destruction of property, but there were always a few violent crimes sprinkled in for flavor. We were on the third of six floors, though, so I felt safe inside the secured building, and viewed these warnings as just another of the newfound charms of city living. I also didn't waste any time getting from my car port to the back door.

I absolutely loved it there.

We had a guy walk right into our apartment once, which was odd considering we were on a middle floor and not even the closest apartment to the stairwell. He waltzed in, plopped on the couch, and lit a cigarette. I was between jobs at the time and had the newspaper want ads spread across the living room floor as I squatted over them, Sharpie in hand. My fearless male protector of a roommate fled to his bedroom at our guest's uninvited entrance, locking the door behind him. Willy Walk-In and I then engaged in a stare down: he blew smoke rings while I tapped the Sharpie against my chin menacingly.

I can assure you, he was terrified. At ninety-five pounds, I was intimidating as hell.

After stamping out his smoke, the visitor opened his mostly toothless face hole and said, "Yo, you got any money?" He was wringing his hands and fidgeting in his seat. My seat, actually, but you know.

"Dude, I don't even have a job." I motioned to the want ads sprawled out around me. "What do you think?"

"You at least got some cans?" See, in the great Mitten state, soda and beer cans have a ten cent deposit, making the sticky ant traps the most widely accepted currency of the ghetto.

"No cans. You got an extra smoke?" I said. I could play this game.

My new friend looked at me for a moment, then grabbed a couple decent-sized butts from the ashtray and showed himself out of the apartment. From that point forward I decided to keep the door locked, and paid closer attention to those cute little notes in the lobby.

In early February I traded in my fiercely protected beer cans for a box of Scooby Doo Valentines, the kind kids give out in grade school, because that's what adults do. That night my roommate and I drank vodka and made out valentine cards for everyone we knew, because nothing says friendship quite like a folded picture of a stoned cartoon dog saying "I Ruv Roo!" I decided Jaime absolutely needed to have one of these cards, so the next day I dropped one in the mail to her, along with a postcard to some vocational school requesting more information on becoming a medical assistant, because it was time to find some sort of direction in my meandering life.

After a few weeks I accused Jaime of being an unappreciative bitch for not sending me an expensive gift basket or something in exchange for my thoughtful card, but she scoffed and said she hadn't received one. The correspondence school hadn't contacted me either, demanding twelve easy payments of $129.95 to transform me into a respectable human being. It became a mystery, the kind it would take four sexually frustrated teens, their dog, a windowless van, and a pound of weed to solve. I got to work on the weed, and waited for the rest to sort itself out.

About six months later I received a letter from the United States Postal Service that contained photocopies of the missing valentine and postcard. Apparently the outgoing mailbox in my building had been robbed, and while my mail had been recovered, it was being held for evidence. Zoinks! It's been well over a decade now and Jaime has changed addresses half a dozen times, but I'm still hoping that someday, maybe when she's taking her last breaths in some dumpy nursing home, that Valentine will find her and brighten her day. Or at least make a suitable coaster for her Ovaltine.

I'd also like to blame the card caper for my lack of professional accomplishments in life. I often lie awake at

It's the Thought that Sucks

night wondering how different my life would be if I had just taken a bullshit correspondence course or two; I bet I'd really have my shit together by now. That mailroom bandit not only stole some letters and a Scooby Doo love wish, he stole my future. Or some shit.

A few years later I was living in a different (but equally shitty) neighborhood, and Jaime was coming to stay with me for her birthday weekend. I was 20 years old and she was turning 22, so as a tribute to our maturity I bought her a set of bath crayons and a My Little Pony.

The gifts were wrapped and left in the guestroom (I was so mature I had a guestroom) with care. The night before Jaime was to come binge drink with me I arrived home from work to find the lock on my back door busted, and a bunch of my shit missing.

The thieves had taken my boyfriend's video game system and all the games, which didn't bother me a whole hell of a lot. The jar of loose change I kept on the counter had been emptied, which was annoying, but not exactly life altering. Some movies were missing and a lot of things were out of place, but we hadn't suffered a huge loss.

The police came and did the whole walk through and pretend to care thing, at which point we went into the guest bedroom and found the wrapping paper on Jaime's gifts had been torn, but once the delinquents saw the contents they'd left them behind. The cops actually tried to dust the half-opened gifts for prints, leaving a nice black, powdery residue on the torn packages.

The worst part of that robbery was I didn't realize until I had put everything back in place and finally settled into bed for the night that the asshole thieves had used *my* pillowcase to haul away my stuff, which was a total dick move.

When Jaime came over the next day I handed her the presents just as the cops had left them, dust and all. Because fuck it, that's why. It didn't matter that she'd get the dust all over herself, because she'd obviously want to take a bath after getting those sweet soap crayons anyway. If anything the forensic treatment made my thoughtful gifts even more special, and created memories that would last long beyond any statute of limitations.

But now it's been over a decade since I bought Jaime a gift, and in that time I have not been the victim of a single petty theft. Coincidence? Maybe. Because I stopped living in shit neighborhoods? Probably. But I'm not about to tempt fate.

Unless, of course, the original Pogo Balls make a comeback. Because nothing could possibly say "Happy 40th Seester, I love you!" quite like a bouncy, Saturn-shaped, hip-shattering death ball. Come at me, Hasbro.

Lame Brain

HOT BOLTS OF PAIN RIP through my chest. I'm fighting for breath, and losing. My fists are clenched so tight that a trickle of blood oozes from my palms. My last coherent thought is an alarm bell blaring through my swirling mind: I'm about to die.

I can't speak. I want to run, to get as far from here as I can before my heart gives out for good, but my legs are too shaky. I'm running out of time. I don't want to die here. I don't want to die at all.

I cross my arms around my waist and curl my body in, making myself small. If I can't run away, I need to hide. But there's no hiding from the walls that are closing in, threatening to swallow me alive.

Every muscle in my body is burning, begging to be used, but I'm frozen. There's no escaping it this time. Everything has led to this exact moment, the moment of my death.

It all started with eight words. Eight little words that, when strung together and spewed forth from the lips of a stranger, have left me deathly paralyzed within my own body.

"What can I get you to drink, hon?"

Needless to say, I don't go out to eat very often anymore.

I was diagnosed with panic disorder when I was 23 years old, but I had been having symptoms for a few years before all hell broke loose and my brain decided it couldn't tell the difference between a sabre toothed tiger attack and a routine eaten alive by cancer, I often had shortness of breath and mild chest pain at night. After a few x-rays failed to detect a giant werewolf tumor in my lungs that flared up only at bedtime, my crappy HMO doctor (who I believe moonlighted as an aerobics instructor) shrugged his well-toned shoulders and said I must have asthma, despite a normal spirometer reading. I took my albuterol inhaler, dropped it in the garbage can on the way out of the office, and went on my merry way. A few years later, and a few weeks before my first brain attack (it's a lot like a heart attack, except stupid), the evening wheezing returned, and I started to feel like I was suffocating inside of my house. I'd run outside, take a few deep breaths, and be okay. I blew these incidents off as the result of smoking too many cigarettes, and by daylight had usually pushed the ordeal from my defective little mind.

Until one day I didn't.

It was lunchtime at the busy car dealership where I had worked for a couple of years, and the break room was usually a fun place to fuck off for an hour with my coworkers. My ex-husband Andy was among them, though we were comfortably married at the time. (I never say 'happily married'—in story-telling it's best to avoid using oxymorons.) It was his 29th birthday, so we were all giving him a rash of shit about closing in on 30. I was still at that magical place in my early 20s where 30 seemed distant, and unlikely to ever happen to me.

But then I started feeling… off. The din of laughter from the breakroom became muffled and distorted, like I was underwater. I became obnoxiously self-aware; every breath, every move, seemed labored. I felt like I had to get out of there, but didn't trust my legs to even hold me up. Everyone just laughed and carried on. I wondered how no one noticed that something was very fucking wrong with me.

I finally mustered the courage to excuse myself, and stumbled outside for a smoke. I was hoping to ingest my nicotine alone as I tried to gather my bearings, but my boss, as well as his boss, were already gathered around the buttpost, partaking in the world's last legal joy. It was the 2000s, and everyone who was anyone was still trying to seal their coffin with nicotine stained nails.

I took a couple of quick puffs before realizing it was the absolute last thing my failing body was crying out for, made an awkward excuse to my superiors for not being able to handle an entire cancer stick, and returned to work. At least I tried to.

As I walked into the busy service lane my legs felt wobbly, and my body grew increasingly heavy. The coworker I always relieved when I returned from lunch was a wily old perv named Bill. He had survived two "widow maker" heart attacks, and in the couple of years we worked together we had become a dynamic duo. He wasn't like a father to me, mostly because of the whole perv thing, but he was my closest friend. As I approached him I reached out to grab the cordless phones we had to keep clipped to our pockets at all times, because even taking a shit wasn't a valid enough reason to miss a customer's phone call, and asked him a question I suddenly felt I was quite literally dying to know.

"Bill, how long would you suggest someone deal with chest pains before they see a doctor?"

"I don't know, maybe half an hour?" He clipped both of our phones to my pants; the weight of the Zach Morris-style cordless receivers nearly brought me down.

"So…." I slurred, "not…a month?"

With that sentence I was hit with such a sharp pain in my chest that I fell forward against the counter. Bill swooped in like a veteran firefighter, throwing my arm over his neck as he helped me hobble out of the customers' sightline, and found Andy. He tossed me to him.

"Get her to a hospital right fucking now!" he yelled at my confused birthday boy, stripping me of my phones, and running to tell both Andy's boss and mine that we would be out of commission for a while.

Andy somehow got me into the car, and we sped off to the nearest emergency room. I hyperventilated the entire way, and yelped out pathetic little screams with each shooting chest pain. The only coherent thought running through my racing mind was that I was going to die on the way to the hospital. But I didn't. And I survived the 45 minutes they left me gasping for breath in the waiting room. And I lived through hours and then weeks of testing, heart monitors, blood work, and attempts to return to work that were only met with repeated incidents of imminent death. I spent the six weeks I was granted for disability leave tidying up my affairs, which basically amounted to throwing away all my embarrassing poetry journals leftover from my teenage angst years. After all, I didn't want that shit to be my legacy.

Eventually after all the poking, prodding, testing, and questioning, I was given a diagnosis for all that ailed me: panic disorder.

So, my heart wasn't failing. I didn't have a giant black tumor overthrowing my lungs. It wasn't even vertigo, or the motherfucking flu. I had suddenly caught a nasty case of the bat shit crazies, and for that there's no cure.

Living with anxiety isn't fretting for hours about whether you switched off the coffee pot, and it isn't some adorably awkward social quirk. It's a degenerative disease of the mind, accompanied by severe and all too real physical symptoms, and the never-ending fear of when and where the next panic attack will strike can transform the landscape of everyday life into a raging hell on Earth.

Eventually I began to learn my triggers: events that are likely to throw me into a panic attack, and should thereby be avoided at all costs. But while I was able to give up movie theaters, restaurants, parties, and pretty much all social interaction altogether, one major trigger was a bit trickier to quit: sleeping.

You see, having an overactive imagination for all things catastrophic causes the mind to take note of every minor change occurring in the old skin sock, often inciting panic over otherwise unnoticeable nuances. Just the act of falling asleep can trigger a panic attack; apparently the slight shift in my heart rate when entering sleep mode freaks me right the fuck out. Sometimes I'm halfway across the room and screaming before I even realize I'm awake. Other times I bolt upright and have to fight for a breath, with my chest pounding and my heart misfiring. Sometimes I just go right to sleep, with no complications. It's a nightly game of Russian roulette, and sometimes I think I'd be lucky to catch a bullet.

Another fun side effect of being so in tune (yet so far out of line) with my body that the slightest disruption causes a catastrophic meltdown is that I cannot accurately judge the severity of any unusual symptoms. A runny nose strikes up the same level of alarm as would a severed limb. Because I don't want to be labeled a hypochondriac, I prefer to err on the side of crazy and wait to seek medical attention until I'm certain of imminent death. Even then sometimes I give it a few days, just to be sure. I'd rather die of untreated appendicitis than run screaming to the ER just to find out that my crippling abdominal pain is nothing more than a suppressed fart.

It's a strange thing, getting sick and being told you're crazy. I fought the diagnosis for a long time. I was certain there was something physically wrong with me, something terrible. I'd probably deny it still, if not for the fact that it's been over a decade of debilitating brain attacks and I'm still not dead.

***

A few years later I had the bipolar label thrown at me as well, after a comfy surprise stay at a four-star psychiatric spa. Anxiety, mania, and depression: it's like hitting all sevens on the pharmaceuticals slot machine. I've been prescribed countless different medication cocktails, and the only thing worse than adjusting to the side effects of a new one is riding out the withdrawal symptoms of its predecessor. I had weeks of hallucinations and other oddball shit when I stopped taking Klonopin, and my doctor said later that the withdrawal effects are similar to that of heroin. Obviously that made me feel like a complete badass, and I'd totally get a sick tattoo to commemorate the experience but my inability to sit still for ten minutes without hyperventilating and crying would probably prove to be detrimental to my reputation as a hardcore bitch.

    I haven't exactly embraced my mental inefficiencies, but I have at least learned to laugh about them. Except for when I'm curled up in the fetal position and crying, that is. Although sometimes I laugh then too, because it really freaks people out.

    I spend most of my time either laughing or crying, but what's so great about straddling the emotional midline anyway? Other than, you know, the straddling. But I think I'd rather dry hump despair than mediocrity any damn day, if it keeps me living in the moment. Because when you live in constant fear of your next brain attack, it's nice to just have something comforting to rub your crotch against.

Domesticated Douchebags

I'M A CAT PERSON. My main ambition in life is to become a shut-in cat lady, and I'm well on my way to making that dream come true. If I ever strike it rich I'm going to buy a huge mansion with an Olympic-sized swimming pool, and then I'm going to drain that bitch and fill it with cat litter, because I'd have so many cats cruising around that scooping their turds would require a hardhat crew and a backhoe.

I've always had dogs in my life as well, but those barking bastards aren't nearly as endearing to me as their kitty counterparts. I mean, dogs are cool and all, but they're way too predictably loyal, loving, and trainable, and I have very little use for that kind of shit.

Cats get a bad rap, but I'm convinced dogs are every bit the assholes that cats are. The difference is cats own that shit. Dogs do dickish things and then try to make up for it by wiggling their butts and sticking their face in your crotch, and if I really wanted to deal with all that I'd just start dating again. But a cat will look you squarely in the eye as it knocks your dinner to the floor right after barfing on your pillow, and how can you not respect that kind of commitment to douchebaggery? I once caught my Chihuahua precariously balanced on three legs on the arm of the couch as he pissed on my coffee table. But after being busted he did the whole head down, "I'm so sorry" thing, as if it were all an unfortunate accident. But when one of my cats jumped onto my bed and whizzed all over my new boyfriend the very first time he spent the night he followed it up by perching proudly on the headboard and licking his paws. In hindsight I probably should have taken that urine bomb as an omen of the failed relationship to follow, but being that I had Bubba's balls removed as a "welcome to my home" gift I didn't really consider him an expert on the art of love.

Dogs are often given way too much credit for their intelligence. My dad once saved his Min Pin's life after finding it in the kitchen, toppled on his side and suffocating, by pulling an empty peanut butter jar off its head. And my acrobatic urinator of a Chihuahua once made sweet love to a baked potato, despite the fact that he was neutered and the potato was, well, a potato.

And then there was Porsche. (Pronounced in uppity prick dialect as Por-sha, because nothing says luxury like a pound dog with defective anal glands and ass blasts that could choke out an entire combat battalion.)

Shortly after my barkaholic Sheltie passed away my house was robbed, and I decided I needed another dog to deter would-be burglars with a cute waggity tail and maybe a raging red rocket. The shelter I visited had only two dogs on site. One was a small puppy that was enthusiastically lapping up a puddle of its own piss, and the other was Porsche.

About a year later I moved from my shitty ghetto neighborhood to a small lake town–my ill-fated attempt at a picket fence existence. (I may not have succeeded, but at least my presence brought down the land value for my ultra-white Bible-humping neighbors.)

One weekday morning, while I was on disability leave for debilitating panic attacks, Porsche and I went for a walk along a wooded trail near our home. The path snaked alongside a small river, which flowed beneath a steep slope at the edge of town. It was a warm spring morning and, as usual, the trail was completely deserted.

The path ended at a narrow wooden dock that extended over a marshy bog. We walked to the end of the dock to sit and enjoy the solitude and sounds of nature awakening for the season.

In other words, I needed a damn smoke.

I lit up and attempted to relax. Porsche, it seemed, had other plans.

I heard a fierce bark, followed by the panicked flapping of wings as a duck took flight. Next came a heavy splash, and suddenly the leash in my hand felt like a fishing line that had snagged a dead hooker.

Only Porsche's head bobbed above the soupy slime; the rest of her was not visible beneath the semi-solid swamp water. Her big, sweet, loving puppy dog eyes stared longingly up at me from the murk, as if to say, "Shit."

I flicked away my smoke and knelt on the dock, grabbed her collar, and pulled. She didn't budge. I was a 90-pound weakling; she was 85 pounds of solid Snausages. I tried to lead her with the leash along the dock, hoping to drag her to shallower "waters" and walk her out of our predicament, but her hind legs were stuck in the muck. I couldn't move her at all.

With a steep hill separating us from the sleeping town, there was no help in sight. It would be another month before winter was declared over and annoying tourist season officially began, flooding the town with yuppies "roughing it" on their yachts with only four bars of signal on their cell phones.

I held the leash tightly as I slid off my shoes and jeans, then lowered myself into the frothy filth. It was waist deep and reeked of stagnant goose shit. Thick slime slithered between my toes, a feeling of absolute yuck I could only compare to waking up in the bathroom of a post-party frat house. The leech scene from the film Stand By Me plagued my mind like, well, a goddamn blood-sucking parasite.

From inside the dungeon of goo I was able to free Porsche's back legs. I hoisted her front paws onto the dock, and pushed her by the butt to safety. I pulled myself up next and sprawled pantsless across the planks. We just laid there for a few minutes, both of us panting way too hard, and exchanged looks that silently implied we'd never speak of this spectacle again. (Well, bitch... I lied).

My arms and legs were coated in silty scum. Only the top of Porsche's head was unsullied. I pulled my pants on over the mud and picked up my shoes, opting to trek back to the homestead barefoot to avoid soiling my sweet ass Payless kicks.

Then Porsche's instinctive canine asshattery kicked in, and she shook her giant body so violently that she showered me head to toe with the fetid film. I had it dripping from my nose, crusted in my hair, and caked in my belly button.

We made the long walk home in silence with our heads lowered in shame. And wouldn't you know it, we passed about fifteen hikers on that return trip, all of them clearing a wide path for the stinky hobo girl and her filthy pooch.

When we finally got home I threw Porsche in the back yard so I could get myself cleaned up first. I peeled my clothes off in the entryway and hobbled to the bathroom. It took two showers and four doggy baths to get the river smell off of us, or to at least cause minimal eye watering, and through it all Porsche peered up at me with her head lowered, apologizing through her big innocent eyes.

Once I was finally satisfied with our stenches I went to pick up my soiled clothes, and smack in the middle of the heap was a steaming fresh cat turd. I looked behind me and there stood Bubba, smirking and licking his paws.

"Fuck you, I'm a cat."

A Crock of Meconium

MOST MOTHERS DESCRIBE PARENTING as a treasured gift; a beautiful, ever-evolving sea of magic and wonder, to be embraced as the greatest blessing that could ever be bestowed upon a mere mortal, carefully cataloguing every moment into their mind's memory reel, not taking a single breath for granted.

Those bitches can go fuck themselves.

I'm an okay mom. I do many of the right things, for mostly the wrong reasons. Good moms massage ointment onto their child's sore anus without thinking twice about it, because a parent's love knows no bounds. I'll apply the ointment all right, but only because my need for the child to quit whining and go the fuck to sleep is only slightly stronger than my desire to not touch someone else's butthole.

I refuse to swear in front of my kid, despite having the mouth of a deranged trucker, but I only hold back because I'm too lazy to deal with the angry phone calls that would pour in if my progeny unloaded a profanity-laden tirade of twatwafflery onto an unsuspecting playmate. But I have paid the price for this preference, as the last time I dropped something heavy onto my foot I screamed out "Boogers!" which is about as therapeutic as icing a fresh bullet wound with a lukewarm Capri Sun

And I'm sorry to pop anyone's snot bubble here, but there is *nothing* magical about childbirth. It's a nasty goddamn shit show, and I mean that quite literally. Pooping during delivery is common, and with all of the alien junk being pushed from the body (the grimy, potato-like infant included), a little feces is probably the least disgusting excretion a new mother might encounter.

My own grisly passage into motherhood started on a Saturday evening, shortly after my boyfriend had waltzed in the front door shit-balls drunk. To be fair, my labor was premature, but that didn't stop me from ripping him a new asshole while snotty blood seeped out of my snatch. We got to the hospital and my cervix was fully effaced but only dilated to one centimeter, and you have to get to ten before it's baby time, otherwise it's like trying to push a marble through a Capri Sun straw.

Sorry, I spend a lot of time doling out bagged beverages these days.

The triage nurses, who I'm pretty sure are paid bonuses based on how many miserable mothers-to-be they turn away, had me waddle the hospital's halls for a couple of hours to see if labor would progress. But walking was misery, I was still pissed at the boyfriend stumbling along beside me, and at one AM Sunday I was no further dilated than when I'd arrived. I was sent home with a sleeping pill and orders to take it easy, which really put a damper on my plans to spend my Sunday jazzercising, but I promised the nurse I'd try to deal.

Of course we couldn't remember where the hell we had parked, and my water broke as we wandered around the hospital's parking ramp.

It didn't happen like it does in movies. An amniotic tsunami didn't gush out of my crotch. I didn't break down into Lamaze breathing, or feel the need to lay down and push. Instead I paused for a moment and wondered if I had just pissed myself, which seemed like a fitting conclusion to the night from hell.

A Crock of Meconium

"I think my water just broke," I said to Scott, after internally assessing the condition of my bladder, which was still full. It was *always* full.

"Should we go back in?" He was mostly sober now, so I guess the hours of hall walking had at least been of some benefit.

"Nah, fuck it," I said. My giant tummy was grumbling. "Let's get some Taco Bell."

We found the car and hit up the drive thru on our way home. I ate my precious Chalupa, then camped out on the couch with a towel tucked into my panties.

Magical, indeed.

Throughout the day the contractions intensified and came at closer intervals, and by five o'clock that evening they were measuring five to six minutes apart. If you've never felt a contraction, just picture being fisted by Edward Scissorhands. We went back to the hospital for round two. The triage Nazis confirmed my water had indeed broken, and they begrudgingly wheeled me to the labor and delivery ward. I wouldn't be leaving without a baby.

My assigned nurse was a bit pissy at me for not returning to the hospital for sixteen hours after my water had broken, but when she checked my dilation situation I had only progressed to one and a half, and she warned that we were probably in for a long one. When she asked if I would be attempting a natural birth or wanted an epidural, I gave her my prepared response: "Bring me all the drugs you can find." She laughed at first, but I raised my eyebrows and stared her down until she realized I was dead fucking serious. She told us the anesthesiologists would be on standby, but I would have to wait until I was dilated to three. Apparently if you're not feeling soul crushing pain the body can lose interest in the whole snatch-stretching process, because magic.

Since my water had been broken for so long there was a moderate risk of infection if I was fingered too frequently, so my cervix would only be checked every two hours. Otherwise Scott and I would be left alone to bask in the anticipation of becoming parents, which we spent watching that one championship sportsball game that I'm not allowed to call by name, lest any profits from this book be sacrificed to the pigskin gods, who will use it to fight concussion lawsuits.

At my next probing I was only dilated to two, and my nurse suggested I take advantage of the whirlpool tub in my birthing suite, because soon I'd be attached to an IV pole dripping antibiotics. The warm bath felt nice but I was still in a lot of pain, and my anxiety was growing. I had gone through intensive therapy in preparation for labor and delivery. Having panic disorder, from the moment I found out I was pregnant I was terrified of having a panic attack during childbirth and fucking the whole thing up. Scott sat by the bathtub and tried to soothe me, but the heat was making me lightheaded, so after fifteen minutes I decided I wanted to get out. Scott switched off the jets, but the bubbles kept rising.

Scott stared at me, his head turning sideways like an intrigued puppy. I stared stoically back. We both knew damn well where those bubbles were coming from. Up to this point in our relationship I had never farted in front of him; but here I was, fat and naked, ripping ass like a trucker on an all-bean diet. We both started laughing, and the harder I laughed the faster the bubbles rose. I was soon floating in a bubbling sea of my own flatulence, and it was exactly the comedic relief I needed to get my head back on straight.

After Fartfest '08 Scott helped me out of the tub and into a fresh hospital gown, and then I was ushered into bed, where the IV of antibiotics was started. I was told to get comfy, because I wouldn't be going anywhere for a while. (Saying "get comfortable" to a person in labor is kind of a bitch move, by the way. You'd might as well tell a four-limb amputee to do the hokey pokey.)

Finally, at one o'clock Monday morning, I was dilated to three; I was finally getting my goddamn epidural.

While I knew from the beginning that I wanted all the drugs the hospital was willing to dole out, I did have a lot of

A Crock of Meconium

anxiety regarding the epidural. I had no real problem with long needles being jammed into my spine; what could possibly go wrong with that? But the thought of the lower half of my body being numb did freak me out a little. But my mental over preparation paid off, and when my extremities went dead I felt nothing but relief.

That is, until I started shivering.

I wasn't cold, but my entire body began trembling, and I couldn't control it. Cue the dreaded panic attack.

My nurse laid two, then three warm blankets on me, but the shivering only intensified. My chest started pounding, and I couldn't catch my breath. When I have a panic attack I *have* to move; every muscle in my body screams to be used, to get away from wherever I currently am, and staying still only intensifies the tortuous symptoms.

But my legs were numb, and I had a tube in my back.

I freaked out. The anesthesia nurses were called back to my room. I was flailing all around, and they were concerned that I was not only going to rip the epidural out, but seriously injure myself in the process.

"I'm going to give you a shot of Stadol to help you relax," my nurse said. I didn't know what that was, but suddenly I was terrified of having any more drugs flowing through me. I tried to plead with her, but all that came out of my mouth was gibberish. The syringe went into my IV, and within seconds my head began to swim.

"Now lay back and get some rest," the nurse said.

The Stadol fucked me up more than any street drug I'd ever taken. In no time at all I felt like Keith Richards with two broken legs. I wasn't able to form words, so after a stoned game of charades I got Scott to set up my iPod and I laid back and listened to Pink Floyd while my chest continued to pound from anxiety. Scott curled up on the sofa and went to sleep. Fucking prick.

At five AM I was only dilated to four. My nurse called my doctor, begging to pump me full of drugs to speed things up (probably so she wouldn't have to listen to my whiny ass anymore), but my doctor told her to give it two more hours. I was entering potential "emergency C-section" territory, so even my cup of ice chips was confiscated so I'd have nothing in my stomach to projectile vomit in the event of going under anesthesia. The last thing I had eaten was that godawful Taco Bell over 24 hours ago, and I was starving. I was catheterized so I wouldn't piss all over myself and the bed in my numbed and drug addled state.

Magic!

My iPod battery died and I was left to listen to the germinator of my misery seed snoring peacefully, and as I debated whether or not to chuck the useless music player at his forehead, some-thing strange happened.

I had been feeling the contractions a bit more over the last few minutes, and worried my epidural was wearing off. But then I squirted... and not in the good way.

I was mostly numb, but I clearly felt a burst of fluid shoot out of my crotch and land near my feet, the trajectory only pulled downward by the blanket tented over my lower half, otherwise I think I'd have splattered the windshield of the International Space Station.

"Well, that's new," I mumbled to myself since the inseminator was fast asleep, and wondered whether I had just projectile pissed or if a magical pregnancy geyser had just erupted from my vagina. But before I could scientifically analyze my alien secretion the contraction pain intensified by a thousand, and when the nurse came back in to check me I was dilated to ten. It was go time.

My doctor hadn't even been on her way yet, so I was asked to cross my legs to keep my miracle in just a little bit longer. Meanwhile the room filled up with nurses, nurse's aides, students, and any hobo passing by the hospital who wanted to come in and take a gander at my crotch cannon. Scott was roused from his slumber, and instructed to hold my hand and try to keep me calm. He was terrified to get near me, and rightly so.

A Crock of Meconium

The doctor finally showed up, and after roughly a thousand hours of pushing she was able to see our baby's head.

"Look at all that hair!" she said, as I heaved through the contraction.

"Do you want a mirror so you can see?" the nurse asked, at which point I wished I could shoot another vagina death sploosh right into her eye.

"Just fucking grab it and pull!" I grunted.

Scott, however, fell for the old "check this out!" trick, even though we had agreed beforehand that he'd stay starboard. He snuck a quick glance and winced, returning to my side as a changed man. Or at least a slightly greener one.

A few million pushes later, it finally happened; my doctor ripped the baby head first out of my snake jaw vagina, then flopped the grimy purple mutant potato onto my chest. She was tiny and squishy with a head full of spiky black hair, and I had never seen anything so perfect. As I laid there in a stagnant pool of afterbirth, holding the mushy little monstrosity that had just tunneled its way out of my shame cave, I reflected on the last eight months, and how this tiny alien had become my whole reason for living, and how magical those first moments as a mother really are.

And then I demanded someone get me a goddamn cheeseburger.

I'm proud to say that I didn't poop while giving birth, but that's probably just because the Taco Bell had cleansed my system out well before I made it to the delivery table. Anyway, all of that superiority I felt over the birth-bed shitters went out the window when, a week or so later, my still stretched pelvic muscles caused me to shit my pants while rocking my screaming demon to sleep.

My little premature pootie muffin had some health complications and stopped breathing four times during her first four days outside the womb. Eight years later, I still sneak into her room at night and place my head against her chest so I can feel it gently rise and fall. I typically trip over an errant headless Barbie doll on my way out, so her peaceful slumber is probably filled with the sound of mommy grumbling "Ouch, boogers!"

The thing is, catering to a tiny and unreasonable little shit machine twenty four hours a day is not a job brimming with unbridled joy. It's both aggravating and terrifying, and puts you in too close of contact with bodily fluids you never even knew existed. And as they get older their heartaches become your heartaches, and you struggle to find your own identity again once the little shitstain no longer needs you every second of every day.

And then, someday, you'll be goofing off with your young child, and discover they have a personality that is uniquely their own. They have their own hopes and dreams, the world is their oyster, and the sky is the limit for this perfect little life you created, and you realize that being this small human's parent is the best thing that has ever happened to you. And then that sweet little crotch blossom turns to give you a kiss, and elbows you right in the goddamn tit.

Boogers!

Breast is Meh at Best

OF ALL THE CHOICES EXPECTANT mothers must make, nothing brings out the armchair vaginabacks quite like the decision on whether or not to breast feed. So it came as no surprise when, upon preparation for my own vaginal annihilation, my breasts became a popular topic of conversation among anyone and everyone that came within gawking distance of my expanding abdomen.

"You ARE going to breastfeed, right?"

"Breast is best. You DO want the best start for your baby, don't you?"

"Formula fed babies are much more likely to develop behavior disorders in adolescence. You know that, right?"

"Your child will undoubtedly develop syphilis of the anus if you don't shove your tits in its face every ten minutes for the first eight years of its life. Do you really hate your baby that much???"

It seemed everyone had an opinion about what I should do with my suddenly voluptuous bosom but me. I knew I didn't want to be the borderline creepy breastmilk crusader that force feeds from her titspring into toddlerdom and beyond. You know the type: Little Johnny asks for a quick snack from mommy's milk muffins in his perfectly enunciated, post-pubescent man voice on the way to pick up his date for the prom. But for the genuine, not-even-remotely-weird little bitty baby phase, I was indifferent. We all know breastfeeding is natural, and I will forever fight for every woman's right to whip out their drippy tits wherever and whenever they need to. Seriously, whatever softcore nudity it takes to make that little shit machine stop screaming is just fine by me. But boob warriors everywhere are just going to have to get used to a few agape mouths and uncomfortable stares. Food is food, boobs are boobs, and both turn men into driveling idiots.

But the boob cheerleaders, ostracized as they are, have managed to vilify formula feeders the world over, making it kind of difficult to be sympathetic to their plight. I've even heard people place blame for both physical and psychological ailments in adulthood on whether or not said sufferer was breastfed as a child. While there may very well be some long term health benefits to tit suckling, some of these are a bit of a reach. Can all-growed-up Little Suzie really blame her irritable bowel syndrome that emerged in her 30s on her mother sticking only synthetic nipples into her little maw? Can teenaged Timmy blame his chronic jock itch on his parents' refusal to use cloth diapers? As soon as the human genome project pinpoints the neglected breast milk gene that goes postal and lays waste to any bitch-ass organ that gets in its way I'll become a believer in the almighty breast… but until then, calm your tits. Literally.

So when it came time to make the decision on whether or not to breastfeed my own child, I ignored the propaganda and focused only on the data that was crucial to me, and that was cost. Formula is fucking expensive; I figured if my boobs could play both dairy farm and cash cow, what was left to consider? The decision was made: I would become a great and powerful breastfeeder.

After 36 hours of premature labor, my little girl entered the world in February of 2008. Her bassinet was proudly stickered with the label "BREAST FED" so the nursery attendants would know to wake me every five fucking minutes to feed her, and so she could feel superior to those unloved, underprivileged, doomed from birth "FORMULA FED" future serial killers the next row over.

Everything was fine and good, until the lactation consultant waltzed into my hospital room, took one look at my lumpy and exposed post-partum body, and announced in a pissy, overworked tone, "You have inverted nipples."

Umm, what?

My barely A cup chesticles had been a source of ridicule all of my life for their size (or lack thereof), but were they actually deformed?

It turns out such a condition isn't necessarily a show stopper for the dairy deluge, but it does add difficulty to the fine art of breastfeeding. And anyone who tells you it isn't a fine art is a goddamn liar; that shit is *hard*.

My nipples were fitted with a rubberized "adapter" that used suction to pop those babies out into play mode when properly attached, and baby Dee was basically suckling a bottle top that happened to be painfully pulling at my girls. All natural, indeed.

As I mentioned before, my daughter was a preemie. I spent the two days after her birth in the care of much friendlier nurses than that first nipple-bashing whore, all the while getting a good handle on the setup process for my fancy European adapter nursing method, but it all went to piss after we were discharged.

I say piss because my proudly breastfed baby turned goddamn yellow.

Our first full day home was pure chaos, as I'm sure it is for all new parents. We had no clue what we were doing. The baby wanted to eat every five seconds, and would suck away for only a few minutes and then fall asleep. My boobs hurt and got so heavy I was sure they'd finally rip from my body in a violent shower of milky blood that would rain down colossal (and colostrum) ruin upon all of us.

And, as mentioned above, the baby's skin turned fucking yellow.

While not much of a mother yet, and with a history of being an epically shitty babysitter (you get a kid stuck in a clothes dryer ONE time), I still knew that putrid urine color was not the sign of a healthy, flourishing newborn.

I called my pediatrician's office in a panic, exclaiming to the nurse that my boobs were broken and my baby was literally a lemon. They were kind enough to see us right away, drawing blood from Baby Dee and sitting me and my swollen sweater puffs down with yet another lactation nurse.

The nurse felt me up a little and said my breasts were engorged (I thanked her for noticing), and despite my soaked shirts the kid wasn't getting much, if any, nourishment from them. She recommended supplementing the baby's diet with formula, and pumping my breasts to relieve some of the pressure. I was also fitted with a small tube to slide into my fancy nipple adapter that would act as a straw to double the child's milk intake before she inevitably suckled herself off to sleep, because preemies have the attention span of narcoleptic kittens. So enters another medical modification required to keep feeding my kid *au naturel*.

 So we bundled up our little pee pee princess and went home to try out the new equipment. I was too exhausted to make mental notes of the details, but I'm sure they could make a sitcom about new parents struggling to figure out how to use a hand pump on defective tits and it would be the next Home Improvement, mainly because it wasn't all that funny and there was a lot of nonsensical grunting involved.

Eventually my boyfriend went out to grab some non-boob originated food for the two of us, and I attempted to give the kid her first bottle of formula. She drank it down like a freshman at a kegger, and projectile vomited it back at me in much the same way. Shortly after being showered in bile-enriched Enfamil the phone rang. It was the pediatrician's office; my daughter's blood work had come back and her bilirubin level was so elevated they were arranging to have her admitted to the hospital immediately. They told me not to freak out (*!!!*), but her jaundice was at a level where permanent brain damage could occur if she wasn't treated right away. At this point, of course, my amber-skinned angel drifted off to dreamland and I couldn't wake her.

In the grips of a full-fledged ugly cry I called my boyfriend and demanded he get home immediately. His car had broken down in the middle of the road and he was trying to push it into a parking lot. Naturally. He probably couldn't decipher from my wailing what the hell I was saying, but figuring it had to be bad when I sounded like a wounded hyena, he abandoned the vehicle and literally ran home. We packed Sleeping Poopy into our other car, and hauled ass for the hospital.

An exhausting two days of alternating boob icing and pumping in front of the ultraviolet aquarium that housed our daughter followed, in which time she slept so hard that she stopped breathing four times. Her diet became primarily formula, supplemented in a bottle with what little breast milk my tiny titbits were able to produce. I had given up on trying to feed her directly from the breast; we needed to accurately measure how much nourishment she was actually taking. Naturally.

After a couple of days in the artificial tanning bed my kid's skin returned to a more normal pigment, and we were sent home for another go – this time with a hospital-grade mammary milker. And after a few go rounds with the expensive tit juice extractor I decided, as any good parent would… fuck this shit. Within two weeks I ceremoniously threw the entirety of the bullshit breast feeding apparatus I had acquired into a snowbank and became a full-fledged fan of formula feeding, as well as of the occasional mom coma. Because there's simply no reason to wake the life giver every half an hour when dad is equally as capable of mixing a goddamn bottle.

And despite that rough first week, my baby girl has grown into a delightful, completely un-yellow kid that is showing no signs of becoming a deranged criminal, despite the wicked formula that coursed through her unloved, underprivileged veins during that formative first year.

When my daughter was five she asked me what boobs were for, and I told her that moms had boobs so they could feed their babies. The look of sheer horror on her face when she asked me if I had fed her with mine cancelled any guilt I may have been harboring over my failure as a dairy farm. Seriously, the militant 'breast is best' crusaders should look at the psychological damage inflicted on adolescents from discovering they spent their early days with their mom's tits jammed into their mouths; I think the data would be decisively in formula's favor.

I never knew if I was breastfed until I was facing the decision on whether to do it myself, and honestly I felt a twinge of relief when I learned my lips never touched my mom's nips. I may not be the ideal poster child for bottle feeding, but hey, my sister turned out all right, and she was formula fed too. 50/50 ain't bad odds, y'all.

Eventually my bruised, bursting B-cups returned to their barely A status, and all was right in the world. And more importantly, curve lovers can now poke fun at my natural unbustiness with accusations that my pathetic tits could starve a baby to death, and they'd be right. But at least I'm no longer rubbing udder cream on my chaffed blinkers.

And despite failing the breast test, I think I'm still a pretty damn good mother. Now where's my vodka? I have a birthday party to put on.

Same Shit, Different Shoes

A COOL THING ABOUT PARENTING is you never know exactly what will end up scarring your child for life. One thing is certain, though: something will. Some asinine little thing that seemed stupid at the time is going to fuck with grown-up Junior the rest of his or her days, and about all you can do is help them work through the big shit so they'll have mostly good things to say about you when they inevitably wind up in therapy.

Of course, as a parent, you do everything you can to prevent those psychiatric visits down the road. You'd move heaven and earth to make sure your sweet child never feels pain, loss, or hunger. You remind them a hundred times a day that you love them so they'll never, ever forget. You sacrifice things that used to matter just to spend more time with them, because you realize that togetherness matters a lot more. You build up their self confidence at every turn by telling them repeatedly that they are beautiful, special, and smart, and instill kindness by teaching them to seek out the good in others. And still, despite everything, some little nugget along the way is going to get lodged in the deep, dark recesses of their sweet little baby brain, and BAM! Your perfectly innocent angel from heaven becomes *jaded*.

Parents are trained from the moment they first hear the little heartbeat, that miraculous little *th-thump* that is completely dependent on them, to live in a state of perpetual fear. The baby's crib is trying to kill them; their food might be laced with poison; every stranger you meet will try to steal them if you're not diligent every second of every day. You spend so much time worrying over the devastating, yet highly unlikely, freakshow shit that the seemingly harmless mild traumas pass right on through, unabated.

The second law of thermodynamics states that a system will only become more disordered over time, and if ever a scientific theory belonged in a psychology book, this is it. Because while that measly little crumb of entropy may be easily passed over, its detrimental effect on the fragile psyche of your precious prepubescent will grow and grow, until it becomes a full-fledged aberration; the arch nemesis of a sound mind. Or perhaps, if you're lucky, it will evolve into just a small, annoying insecurity that will plague their pitiful brain for the rest of their semi-functional days.

The main problem, though, is that it's a fucking crapshoot to determine what insignificant occurrence will wind up being so goddamn traumatic that Tiny Tim is still losing sleep over it in his golden years. It could be hurtful words hurled out of anger, or the tragic death of a beloved cartoon character. They may never get over the loss of an eternally misplaced stuffed animal, or that of a beloved booger flicked long before its time.

For me, it was shoes.

When I was in second grade, which just so happens to be the current age of my daughter, my parents were freshly divorced. My mom, sister, and I had just moved from our sprawling farmhouse into a cramped single-mom shack. We had to get rid of our dog, and all but two of our cats (at last count we had been up to fourteen, all outdoors and freely breeding). For being only seven years old, my life was a fucking mess.

But despite all of her troubles, both emotionally and financially, my mom held it together like a goddamn champ, and thanks to her strength I suffered very few of the ill effects associated with living through a "broken" home. However, in all of her efforts to make sure I never felt the sting of my dad's absence, the stress of how we would afford groceries, or the psychological damage of divorce, one day she *did* neglect to make sure I had matching shoes on my fucking feet.

So the two shoes on my two feet had originated from two different pairs. Big deal, right? Punky Brewster did that shit all the time, and she was cool even *before* her chest ballooned into double D's. Besides, both were primarily white tennis shoes, so, easy enough mistake to make. One had purple laces, while the other was fastened with pink Velcro; close enough. They had something else in common, though: the heel-toe alignment. That's right; my shoes were not only from mismatched pairs, they were both left feet.

I'm not sure how I waddled down to the bus stop and through half of the morning recess without noticing something foul was afoot, but I honestly had no idea of my faux pas until a bigger kid crucified me in the most merciless of all playground punishments: he pointed at me and laughed.

I limped briskly away from my attacker before the inevitable crowd could form to join in on the taunting, but the damage had been done. And once I was made aware of my error, the embarrassment of it consumed me every single agonizing one of the 23,400 seconds of that school day.

I had no choice but to grit my teeth and get through the day. Nowadays a kid might tearfully scuff down to the school's office, where they could call home, or possibly even get a loaner pair of kicks for the day. My daughter came home once in kindergarten wearing clothes that weren't hers;

there was a note in her backpack stating she had had an "accident" and had been given a donor outfit, and to please wash and return it to the office for the next pants pisser. I was sure she'd be consumed with shame for having a bathroom accident at school, but the incident passed without a single tear shed, and two years later she's no worse for wear.

Meanwhile I can *still* remember which kids wet their pants in my kindergarten class. Those poor, weak-bladdered bastards wore that shame for the duration of their academic careers. At my high school graduation our destined-for-success valedictorian gave an insightful and moving speech, but I'll always remember her best as the girl who pissed herself on the story time rug when we were five.

But at my elementary school in 1988 we didn't even have a school office. It was a rural, five classroom school that housed first through fourth grade. The fifth classroom served as our gym slash music room slash auditorium. Hot lunch service was set up in the school's hallway each day, and we returned to our classroom desks to eat. The school's only phone was located in the tiny kitchen at the very end of the hall, and each week a different fourth grader was selected as the school's secretary, with the obligation of running out of the room and down the hall to answer the phone if it rang. This caused a whole new level of anxiety for me when I reached that age, as I've always suffered from tinnitus (my dad thought it was funny to tell my sister and I to put our ears next to our giant living room speakers as Def Leppard's "Rocket" blasted off), and when it was my turn on phone duty I often ran out of the classroom only to find the phone hadn't actually made a peep.

Back in second grade, though, I didn't have to worry about mucking up such important responsibilities; I was just a pint-sized loser with two left feet.

I spent the rest of that fateful day awkwardly trying to cover one foot with the other, to keep my terrible tennis shoe dilemma from becoming the subject of any further playground mockery. At each recess period I stood alone against the wall of the small school, blinking back tears as I prayed for the bricks and mortar to open up and swallow me whole.

I was certain I would die of embarrassment that day, and I only hoped that the angel of death would swoop in and snatch me sometime before lunch. It was pizza day, and the thought of scarfing down that sauceless cardboard monstrosity while blisters ate away at the squished big toe of my right foot was just too much to bear.

Despite my overwhelming sense of foreboding, I did make it through the school day. The moment I stepped off the bus I ripped the shoes off my feet, found each of their respective partners in the closet, and after pairing them up placed the matching pairs on opposite ends of the house. And as far as childhood traumas are concerned, Shoegate '88 wasn't really that big of a deal. Within a couple of days it had dissipated from the forefront of my mind, making room for a whole new set of trials and tribulations that plague all middle class white children, such as whether to play on the monkey bars or on the swings.

Over the next few years I had much more serious incidents and injuries to plague my developing psyche. I was bit in the face by my neighbor's dog. I fell through the ice into a frigid pond I was playing on and had to trek a half a mile through the snow, soaking wet, to the warmth of home. I came within inches of being smucked by a semi truck when I crossed the street on my bike without first looking both ways.

And now, in my 30s, I harbor no residual fear of dogs. I don't think twice about crossing the street, and it's only the fear of my vagina freezing shut that keeps me from enjoying ice skating, ice fishing, or just being outside in the winter for any goddamn reason at all.

But there still is one thought that haunts me each and every day of my life, and that is whether or not my fucking shoes match.

Every day I check my feet at least five times before I leave the house, and as soon as I get in the car, like clockwork, I reopen the driver's door so the dome light pops on so I can look at my feet one last time before backing out of my driveway. It may not be a huge drag on my quality of life, at least not now, but the experience of showing up to elementary school in mismatched shoes has certainly had a lasting effect. And who knows, in twenty more years I might be drawing little sneakers all over the walls of my padded room while belting out only the "you put your left foot in" verse of the hokey pokey over and over again; only time will tell.

Which begs the question: what little tidbits of my daughter's childhood will stick with her all of her life? Because, at this point, the kid's mind seems unshakable.

I can still remember the first time I saw a penis. I was five or six years old, and my mom's friend had come over with her kids, at least one of which was a boy. I only had a sister, so I had no idea that boys and girls were equipped any differently, other than the whole "sugar and spice" versus "snakes and snails" ingredients in our genetic makeups. But the little boy didn't close the door when he went to the bathroom, and I happened to walk by and see him standing there, peeing. Standing. *To pee.* I was frozen like a deer in headlights, except the headlights were a penis. My mom yelled at me to move, but I couldn't look away; I was mesmerized by the crotch monster before me.

My kid, however, made it through her first penile encounter unscathed.

She went to an in-home daycare five days a week, and the daycare provider had a son that was just two months older than my darling girl. The two kids quickly became the most adorable of best friends.

When that boy was not quite two years old he discovered, as most little boys do, his "pee pee". And, like most boys, he was quite enamored with it.

One day my daughter barged into the room where he was getting his diaper changed.

"Look, pee pee!" he said, pointing excitedly to his unit.

Same Shit, Different Shoes

At this point his mom realized that my daughter was standing there, and hurriedly covered his itty bitty boy bits with a diaper.

Without missing a beat, my girl said "Bye, pee pee!" and blew a kiss to the hastily covered toddler dong.

Needless to say, the girl does not shock easily.

In fact, the child is tough as nails. At seven years old she's endured the loss of loved ones, both people and pets. She's rolled with the changes of a struggling new family that has never been completely sure of where it's going. And despite my best efforts to mask it, she has seen some of the ugliness mental illness can inflict on both a person and a family, yet when I'm completely broken she will throw her arms around me and tell me I'm the greatest mom in the world, and it makes everything a little better.

Still, I know that someday there will be some problem that I'm not able to gloss over for her; it might be some tiny, insignificant occurrence or, God forbid, a full blown calamity, and it will burrow its way into the back of her brain, where it will fester for her entire life. In the meantime I'm going to keep telling her I love her, that she is special, and that there is infinite beauty to be found in this world, if she just keeps looking for it. And to always put her best left foot forward.

Poppin' Bones

"MOM," ROSIE SAYS. "What does it mean to pop a bone?"

I spit coffee across the living room.

"I'm not sure," I reply cautiously. "Where did you hear it?"

"Shane says it all the time, 'I think I just popped a bone.'"

Shane is the biggest boy in her class. I'm not sure he's big enough to sport wood, but by eight years old I'm sure some boys have at least heard such crude terms.

"Um, well, it's a boy thing." I hope this will be the end of it. I should know better by now.

"Why? Why can't girls pop bones?"

"Well honey, boys' bodies are a little different than girls. We've talked about that before."

"But I have bones," she says.

"I know you do, baby." I'm trying to tread lightly, but curiosity has gotten the best of me. "What does Shane do when he says that? What is he referring to?"

"Well he puts a pencil in his clothes, so it's sticking out. And then he says 'I just popped a bone.'"

This time the coffee nearly erupts from my nose.

"That's highly inappropriate," I manage to spit out between giggles. "He shouldn't stick pencils down his pants."

"Pants?" Rosie looks confused. "No, he sticks it in his shirt sleeve. And then says 'Uh oh, I think I popped a bone.'"

Are you fucking kidding me.

I'm two seconds from explaining erections to my eight year old daughter, and this kid is only playing about having a broken arm?

"Oh, he's pretending he broke his arm. He's just being silly." Whew! Crisis averted!

"Oh." I see the wheels turning behind her big brown eyes. "Mom?"

"Yes, dear?"

"Why did you think he had the pencil in his pants?"

Fuck.

Speed Freak

I'VE ALWAYS DESPISED AUTO racing. Especially NASCAR. It's painstakingly boring to watch, a pointless waste of fossil fuels, and so stereotypically redneck that they might as well open each race with The Beverly Hillbillies theme song instead of the national anthem. But despite my malevolence toward the so-called sport, I once rode shotgun in a race car going 174 miles per hour around one of the most famous tracks in the world.

It was a classic case of 'it sounded fun at the time' that came back around to bite me in the ass many months later, and further proof that what you decide in Vegas should be done in Vegas, before you have the chance to sober up and get scared shitless.

I had surprised my then-fiancé Scott (who is now my husband, and therefore referred to in much more profane terms) with a trip to Las Vegas for his birthday. Being a gearhead with a boner for all things motorsports, he decided a visit to Las Vegas International Speedway should be on our vacation agenda. It sounded stupid to me, but I figured I could handle a few minutes feigning interest about a paved oval in between jackpots. After a quick web search he discovered that our visit just so happened to coincide with a "special" event at the racetrack: The Richard Petty Driving Experience.

The Richard Petty Redneck Extravaganza is held at only a handful of tracks on the NASCAR circuit. For the measly price of an arm and half a leg it offers fans the option of riding in a real NASCAR death machine with a professional driver, or sit through a few hours of instruction and actually get behind the wheel.

It's like Space Camp, but for morons.

Scott's discovery of this "once in a lifetime!" opportunity was met with an eye roll and an unenthusiastic jerk-off motion of the wrist by me, but then again so was his marriage proposal and that didn't really deter our liquor-soaked nuptials much. He was bound and determined that he was going to drive a damn race car, and since the vacation was a present to him to begin with, I told him to go ahead and book it. What were a few hours out of my day, anyway? Besides, maybe I'd just stay at the casino while he went and played his little game of redneck hero; no skin off my ass. Or so I thought. It turned out that by paying the ridiculously high price they charge a person to potentially kill themselves in a fiery crash, they dole out a free ride along ticket. What a deal!

Of course he told me I didn't have to take the free ticket. He'd either use it himself, or let it lapse. It's not like we paid for it. But he wanted me to go with him to the track, so I figured the least I could do was have a little thrill ride of my own. After all, if you're going to go to Hillbilly Heaven, you may as well enjoy the ride.

I was so fixated on the rest of our trip that I didn't really give the whole racing adventure much thought. It was my first trip to Vegas as an adult. I had gone once when I was 12, I'm assuming only because my parents couldn't find a babysitter. And let me tell you, you learn *a lot* about life wandering the Vegas strip as a pre-teen. You also get handed a lot of pornography, but that's a topic I'm still working through with my therapist. As for the Vegas death ride, I figured I'd give Scott his afternoon of auto-erotic enjoyment and the rest of the week would be about booze, bets, and bad decisions. The shit that *I* liked.

Speed Freak

Our not-so-eagerly anticipated hayseed holiday was scheduled for our second full day in Vegas, followed by reservations at a major sportsbook for a big game I'm not allowed to refer to by name on the following day. The rest of our itinerary was intentionally left blank, as commitments aren't really our thing. That's probably why we both sped up our steps every time we stumbled past a quickie wedding chapel while in Sin City; climbing into race cars and throwing all our money down on the underdog team was fun, but we weren't about to do anything crazy.

We flew into The Neon City late Thursday night, and after making our way through the glitz, glam, and gonorrhea to our hotel, had a couple of celebratory drinks and slot pulls. Since we were up until the wee hours, sleeping in on our first day of vacation was a must. We took our time prying the crust from our eyes, savored our coffee, took long, relaxing showers, and hit the strip running at a leisurely ten o'clock on Friday morning. Unfortunately, we were still operating on Michigan time. Locally it was only seven in the damn A.M., and while New York is the city that never sleeps, Vegas is the city that woke up with one hell of a hangover and isn't going to get its ass moving much before noon.

Nothing opens in Vegas before ten. Nothing. Unless, of course, it never closes in the first place. We have plenty of twenty-four-hour casinos in Michigan, but they lack that one thing that makes the seedy desert oasis so damn alluring: free booze. You can get anything you want to drink if you just drop a nickel or two into a slot machine every few minutes. So for about three hours we wandered from casino to casino, dropping coins and downing mimosas.

As we stumbled our way down the strip, Scott's redneck radar zeroed in on the one damn attraction that didn't involve booze or bets, the NASCAR Café (note: said café was demolished in 2013, which should prove my point about its appeal). A pitiful roller coaster track jutted out from inside the building, formed an upside-down loop, then disappeared around the side of the building. A large sign ominously proclaimed the dainty coaster SPEED: The Ride. Scott couldn't resist going inside the cafe, and I was the perfect level of drunk to entertain myself by making fun of the place. Besides, there was a roller coaster…albeit a small and ridiculous one.

We were nearly the only ones inside the glorified arcade, which is further testament to its dismal fate. There were a few race artifacts around, but otherwise it was just video games and slot machines with the NASCAR logo slapped across them. They also had a driving simulator that had Scott's gearhead glands salivating.

Since Scott was going to waste perfectly good gambling money on a stupid thrill ride, I decided I'd do the same and conquer the little rollercoaster. We bought our tickets but neither attraction was open yet (big surprise) so we played a few moronic games while we waited. Eventually Vegas woke up, took a piss, downed a bloody mary, and was back in business.

I made my way through the empty snake line of the coaster (wishful thinking, eh NASCAR Café?) and waited. Since we were first I hadn't seen the ride actually go yet, but I had a pretty good idea of how lame it was. The ride literally started a few feet before the track exited the building and made the loop. I'd pulled off more daring feats on my tricycle.

The ride operator held us up for about ten minutes, waiting for more riders. While a rush of thrill seekers for this sad excuse for a ride seemed unlikely, a few more stragglers did wander in. I can only assume they were lost, and thought the coaster was some sort of trolley to somewhere less shitty.

I boarded the adorable little train of terror and pulled the shoulder harness down. Scott, standing behind the boarding "line" (all four of us that wanted to ride the stupid thing were already on it), got his camera out to take my picture. I stuck out my tongue and made a jerk-off motion, because I'm photogenic like that.

In all my inebriated ridiculing of Speed: The Ride I never once paused to think about its name. That it maybe held just a tiny morsel of significance. All I saw in my drunken haze was the diminutive track and the lame NASCAR logo. So you can imagine my surprise when, mid-wrist wank, that fucking coaster took off like a goddamn bullet on meth.

I saw Scott's jaw drop in silent yet hysterical laughter, and my stomach stayed behind to keep an eye on the platform. Meanwhile my body went full throttle through that not-so-ridiculous loop, and then to the part of the track that I couldn't see from outside, which was basically a nearly ninety-degree incline into nothing. The train climbed and climbed, and just when I thought we were going to run out of track and go shooting into the sky, the upward motion slowed the coaster's momentum. For a moment we seemed to hang there, staring straight at the desert sky – and then gravity kicked in, and the train slid backwards down the vertical track, back through the loop, and back into the building. We slammed back right where we had started, and while less than thirty seconds had gone by, I learned a lot. Mostly I learned that I was a giant pussy, and maybe speed-related thrills weren't my thing.

When the shoulder harness lifted I wasn't sure I could lug my ass out of that seat, but out of the kindness of Scott's heart he quit laughing long enough to help me out of the demonic contraption and toward another drink. And then he laughed some more.

It rained every single day of our vacation in the desert. The plus side of that was our little Redneckscapade at Las Vegas Motor Speedway was canceled. We managed to have a thrilling day anyway by racing our rented Chevy Aveo through the watered down wasteland to get a soggy look at the Hoover Dam.

As it turns out, however, I was not off the hillbilly hook just yet. Not long after we arrived home to the comfort of the frozen tundra of Michigan, we were contacted by the Richard Petty Driving Experience to reschedule our adventure. And we could use our "rain check" at any other participating track.

The closest track to home is Michigan International Speed-way, but even diehard NASCAR fans will tell you that track is boring as shit. With just a couple more hours of travel time we could live out our farmland fantasy at Indianapolis Motor Speedway, aka The Brickyard.

Kimmy Dee

Scott was all about Indy because it is an iconic, world-renowned track with a rich history spanning over a century, and I was for it because there was a bar in Indianapolis that I really liked. It was a no brainer, which is handy whenever you're dealing with NASCAR enthusiasts.

Two days before we were set to hit the track we were emailed the forms we needed to fill out prior to setting foot anywhere near the race cars. These "forms" were basically just waivers, stating that we were entering these death machines of our own free will, and that our charred corpses couldn't sue anyone if (or when) we perished in a fiery crash. It was while perusing these standard issue accidental death documents that I had my first race-related panic attack. Visions of getting my ass handed to me by an itty bitty roller coaster flashed through my brain. But with a shaky hand I scribbled my signature, figuring it was only fitting for me to die doing something I hate.

During the five-hour commute to Speedtown I did all I could to distract myself from the panic threatening to prematurely explode my heart, but there isn't much to do while passing through northern Indiana. You can only play "Guess that Field!" (will it be corn, or will it be beans?) for so long before it loses its splendor. As my dad used to say, the reason they call Indiana "the Crossroads of America" is because everyone is just trying to get the fuck out. And where did he die? Indianapolis.

We arrived at the world's first speedway under aggravatingly sunny skies, and the day's festivities were already well underway. I walked around with Scott for a bit while he geeked out, but luckily we didn't have enough time to kill to check out the Hall of Fame Museum that is located on the grounds. I had come to Indy prepared to die in a heap of twisted metal, not of boredom while staring at carburetors.

Scott had to take a two hour "class" before they let him behind the wheel, because apparently being able to properly identify clutch, gas, and brake were important when you were participating in high-speed suicide. We parted ways at one of the garages in the track's infield, where his crash course (see what I did there?) was being held.

There was no training required for the ride along, though. Just suit up, strap in, and go. The ride-alongs ran all day, with no specific appointment time like the driving experiences. There was a line where the cars for the day were stationed on pit road, all I had to do was make my way to the front of it and be on my merry way around the racetrack a few times. But there was no reason to rush into anything... I had a few hours to kill, after all, and the line of victims err riders wasn't very long. I decided to just observe for a bit, to get an idea of just how painless the whole thing would be. Besides, I was feeling a little queasy. Just some waiver-induced belly butterflies, I figured. I wouldn't let NASCAR defeat me; I had ridiculed this sport's participants and enthusiasts way too much over the years to chicken out. So I'd watch a bit, take my victory laps, wait for Scott to finish playing his silly live action Speed Racer game, and before I knew it we'd be tipping back tequila shots.

I plopped my ass on the infield bleachers behind the pits. Directly in front of me was a group of drivers fresh out of their training, gearing up to get behind the wheel. There were four cars parked on pit road for the driving experience, in two groups of two; the front car of each set would be driven by a professional, and one of the rookies would follow in the second. Scott told me later they were instructed to try to keep within three car lengths of the instructor, which is pretty damn close when you're talking speeds up to 140 miles per hour. (The vehicles for the driving experience were governed so they would go no faster than 140, but there were no such restrictions on the ride along deathmobiles!) Drivers got to cruise around for seven laps, then the instructor would lead them back to pit road and the next newbie would hop in the driver's seat. The takeoffs were staggered so that the front duo was generally about a half a lap ahead of the next.

Just behind this set up on pit road was the ride along line. The ride along consisted of three laps, and since the cars didn't have the speed governor, during those three laps riders would get the added thrill of flying past inexperienced, white-knuckled drivers that could make a fatal error any second. Added bonus!

I sat in the bleachers long enough to see a couple of drivers and a handful of riders do their thing, then struggle to climb out of the cars and stagger away. With each roar of the passing motors the butterflies in my belly batted their wings a little harder. After a few minutes they cut the fluttering bullshit and went straight for their semi-automatic assault weapons, laying waste to my weakened innards, execution style.

Hunched over and holding my aching gut, I toddled my way to the nearest restroom. There probably should have been a priest nearby for what happened next. I'll spare anyone who's actually still reading the gritty details… let's just say that everything I had consumed the past couple of days, plus a stray demon or two, erupted from one end of my body or the other. Or both simultaneously.

While I was a bit preoccupied and not really paying attention to the time, I'm pretty sure the above-mentioned exorcism ate up (and then vomited again) about a half an hour. In all of that time no one else entered the restroom, which was fortunate for all of humanity. What has been seen cannot be unseen, and all that. Eventually both geysers slowed to a trickle, so I did what I could to freshen up before making my walk of shame back to the racetrack.

Having survived whatever the hell had happened to me in the bathroom, I decided I was as ready as I'd ever be to take my death ride.

I got in line.

There were about twenty people ahead of me, none of which looked even remotely as terrified as I felt. I was the only one flying solo; everyone else had a friend or spouse to nervously chat to, although there were very few women. I chalked that up to the superior intelligence that came with the extra X chromosome. But there I stood, the superior sex, waiting for a man to drive me head on into a cement wall.

Although I'm generally an introvert that prefers to be left to her own affairs, I do tend to make temporary friends wherever I go, and the line to enter the Podunk Pearly Gates was no exception. I made idle chit chat with everyone around me, although most of my conversational idioms pertained to our imminent deaths.

As the line progressed I was fitted with a flame-retardant jumpsuit, and by "fitted" I mean they found the very smallest one they had, which seemed to have been designed for a 400-pound behemoth. I guess they don't anticipate child-sized weaklings to show up for those gigs. I climbed into the suit, zipped it up, and waddled like a terrified Michelin Man through the remainder of the line.

When I was down to just a few victims ahead of me I heard a familiar voice from behind, taunting me. I turned to see Scott, in a much better fitting jumpsuit, leaning against the fence separating the infield from pit road, just to the side of the ride along line. His instructional period was complete, and now they would be taking turns getting behind the wheel. He had at least a half an hour to wait, though, while my doom was rapidly approaching. I offered to remove myself from the line and sit with him, but he politely declined. And by politely declined, I mean he did some pointing and laughing in my general direction.

Scott stuck around while the line continued to dwindle, which only amplified my panic. I didn't want him to see how ugly I would be when I died. He, however, was enjoying every damn second of my fear. With all the insults I had hurled at him about his NASCAR habit over the years, he was enjoying the hell out of it charging back to kick my lily-livered ass. I'm not sure if rednecks believe in karma; I'm even less sure that they can spell it. Regardless, I refused to let a dumb looking car covered in brightly colored logos for motor oil and snack foods defeat me. I envisioned my eulogy:

Kimmy Dee

Here lies Kimmy. Well, somewhere inside the mangled wreckage of the STP-Mobil-Doritos-mobile. The Pepsi-Quaker State-Twinkie paramedics put forth a great team effort today, but her body was mostly liquefied during the fiery crash comin' offa turn three. But now she's gone through the great golden arches in the sky, and ba-da-ba-ba-ba, she's lovin' it™! Now if everyone will please rise and remove their bandanas, we'll drape a giant Confederate flag over this mess and go get us some ice cold Coors and smoke a few Camels. Yee-haw, and Amen.

The person two spots ahead of me in line was a heavier set woman, and she struggled mightily to get into the car. The race cars don't have doors, you know, so you have to climb in through the window. Two people had to come out and help her, and suddenly I had a whole new fear consuming my whole being: forget going down in a final blaze of redneck glory… what if I fell and broke my ass just trying to get in the damn car? My fear of public humiliation quickly trumped my fear of death, and all that mattered from that point forward was getting into that stupid deathtrap gracefully.

I was pretty sure the agility benefits of my lean physique would counteract my catastrophic clumsiness when it came time to climb into that car, but then they threw a HANS device and helmet on me, and all bets were off.

The HANS (Head And Neck Support) Device straddles a race car driver's (or rider's, in my case) shoulders, and anchors from the helmet are secured to the seat to keep the head level with the shoulders to prevent serious neck injuries in the event of a crash. They became required equipment in NASCAR after Dale Earnhardt Sr. died instantly of a basilar skull fracture in the 2001 Daytona 500, which was the biggest damn tragedy country music radio ever capitalized on, at least until 9/11. I know this because at the time of Sr.'s death I was ear raped by new country music for eight hours a day at my job, and while I had no idea who Dale Earnhardt was before he died, within weeks of his death I was ready to tithe my 401(k) directly to his estate and sing hymns to the divine glory of his mustache.

Safety benefits aside, the HANS device and helmet did a number on my center of gravity; and, in effect, my confidence when it came to getting my ass into that car without looking stupid. I felt less like Bo Duke and more like a drunk Chihuahua with one of those cones on its head, more likely to face plant onto the asphalt than to appear anything in the neighborhood of cool.

And before I could wrap my suddenly elephantine head around what was happening, I was being summoned onto pit road, where my high-velocity chariot of doom awaited.

It was on rubbery legs (and with a ridiculously heavy head) that I made my way to the race car. Still concerned with maintaining my dignity on entrance, I tried to cavalierly lift one leg up over the passenger side window to climb aboard, but with the nervousness and the ridiculous head weight I could barely lift my foot off the ground without nearly tumbling backwards. The worker tasked with getting me strapped into the car saw my struggle, and gave me a boost before I could make too big of an ass of myself.

Once inside the car the driver, wearing the same ridiculous getup as me, said hello and introduced himself, although for all I remember his name could've been Dick Trickle. (It wasn't him, I just couldn't write this piece in good conscience without saying Dick Trickle.) I told him I was nervous and he chuckled, which wasn't all that reassuring. But before I could say anything else the worker that had tossed me into the car fastened my shoulder straps and connected my helmet to the HANS device, leaving me, for all intents and purposes, immobilized. It was like a straitjacket, minus the soothing comfort of a padded room. As soon as I was hooked in the driver started the engine, and it felt like my ribcage was going to rattle right through my skin. He pulled the car forward on pit road, into what served as the starting position for the day's festivities.

At that point, if I hadn't already violently evacuated my bowels not long before, I'm certain I would have shit myself.

Scott was on the other side of the chain link fence separating pit road from the infield. He was recording video of me on his phone while laughing at my panic. I told him I loved him, because I guessed that's what you're supposed to say right before you die. At that particular moment, however, love was the last thing I was feeling. He had gotten me into this bullshit situation, after all.

I asked the driver if he could just, you know, take it slow for me. I tried to bat my eyelashes, but through all of the safety gear I'm pretty sure the effect was lost. He turned to me, not evening bother to feign concern, and jovially said "Nope!" before jamming down on the gas.

I'd like to say that my life flashed before my eyes, or I had some sort of high-speed enlightenment, or even that I screamed bloody murder, but none of those things happened. Mainly because it's goddamn impossible to do any of those things at 174 miles per fucking hour, which was our clocked speed. We did three laps around the two and a half mile track and my stomach felt like it never left pit road. The wind dried out my lips and made the top one curl like some sort of deranged, panic stricken Elvis, while I waved my hands all around because they were the only part of my adrenaline-overdosed body that I could move. We roared up on those slow-moving (140 mph) training cars and whipped around them on the outside as though they were standing still. The wind and the noise and vibration of the engine rattled every single bone in my body. I don't think I took a single breath. I didn't really have time to.

In what felt like no more than a nanosecond we were whipping back onto pit road, seven and a half miles under our wheels. As soon as the ride came to a complete stop my pit road buddy came and unhooked my head and shoulder restraints. My stomach found its way back into my body and I thanked my driver, whoever the fuck he was, and shimmied out of the window with all the grace of a moose on meth; it wasn't pretty, but I made it under my own somewhat euphoric power.

I ventured back to the infield and to Scott, to whom I'm pretty sure I shouted some excited gibberish about my ride, forgetting that he probably wasn't suffering from the same racetrack tinnitus that I was. Not yet, anyway.

Shortly after my ride was done he got to take his drive while I sat in the stands and reflected on how badass I was for surviving such a feat, and also brainstorming ways to deny the fact that the whole experience was fun as hell. Minus the bathroom theatrics, of course.

It wasn't long before we were at my favorite Indianapolis bar, tossing back tequila shots and swapping war stories of our time spent at the Brickyard. But the true culmination of our Richard Petty Driving Experience came long after we had left the track. After last call we stumbled out of the bar only to find ourselves staring down the most alluring of all automobiles that had ever graced either the road or the racetrack: the Oscar Mayer Wienermobile.

A brief photo-op ensued, where I may or may not have enthusiastically licked the grimy metal of the mobile wiener before we took off running, sure that the operators of the fuel-injected phallus would be in hot pursuit.

They weren't.

The next morning we headed for home, with wicked hangovers and fuzzy memories. And I may have even grown a teensy tiny, itty bitty smidgen of respect for the speedturds that manage to operate those race cars at such ridiculous speeds and simultaneously pull off some crazy tricks, like breathing. Mostly, though, I'm just thankful that I got to lick that illustrious wiener.

Ovarian Horror Story

READERS OF MY BLOG ARE WELL aware that I'm not overly impressed with the logistics of being a woman. I don't mentally identify as a male or anything; I'm just really lazy, and owning a vagina is hard work. The basic maintenance and upkeep can be daunting enough, but then you throw in all the laws regulating our unruly crotch pockets, and being the "softer sex" feels more like owning labia-front property policed by the world's strictest (and primarily male) homeowners' association.

I even rebelled against my gender by refusing to grow a respectable set of tits. Some women burn their bras; I took it a step further and just flat out have no need for those mammary-muzzling contraptions of titillating torture. But then my genetically inferior reproductive system really showed me its cunty side.

It began with nagging abdominal pain. At first I chalked it up to just another side effect of the depression/anxiety shitshow that my brain treats me to as an intermission act in between major meltdowns, but after weeks of constant pain and a few nights spent crying in the fetal position because it hurt to move, I decided I'd better suck it up and see my doctor.

(Don't feel too sorry for me here, though; crying in the fetal is actually one of my favorite hobbies. Now if I had an affliction that caused me to mall walk whilst sipping a pumpkin spice latté and swapping super juicy sex stories with members of the Parent Teacher Association, then I would request your sympathy. As well as a mercy killing. But I digress.)

After stealing some of my piss and listening to my bowels (he said they sounded 'normal'—I think 'majestic' would have been a more accurate adjective) my primary care physician ordered an ultrasound of my lady bits in order to make me go away. In his defense, I'm a total pain in the ass patient. Thanks to a traumatic ER experience during my first panic attack I pretty much have to be fully sedated to even have my blood pressure checked, which is apparently counterproductive.

The ultrasound showed a "large, septated mass" on my right ovary, requiring an MRI for further diagnosis. Figuring that the medical field was just fucking with me, I considered putting an end to the whole diagnostic adventure right there. Transvaginal ultrasound? Fine. It's not like I'd never had a lube soaked, condom-cloaked wand shoved up my twat. I *did* go to public school and all. But an MRI was a little too much for this anxiety-plagued fuckwit to endure. But I handled it like a rock star (translation: I took a LOT of pills) and got through it. Two days later (and two days before my follow up appointment with my gynecologist) the clinical report, complete with diagnosis, came in the mail: Ovarian Teratoma.

WebMD defines a teratoma as "A type of tumor that can take on human aspects -- it might grow hair, teeth, or even part of a finger or eyeball."

Dafuq?

The follow up appointment with my gynecologist confirmed it: my abdomen was harboring a growth roughly ten times the size of my ovary that might or might not contain hair, teeth, an eyeball, or even brain matter. As expected, I took this as spectacular news. I mean, if you're going to have a tumor, it may as well be the freakiest fucking thing imaginable, amirite? Some less sadistic medical professionals call this a "dermoid cyst", but where's the fun in that title? I mean, TERATOMA. Like tarantula, only with sharper teeth and GROWING INSIDE YOUR FUCKING BODY.

My doctor scheduled surgery to have the alien invader, as well as whatever other lady bits needed scooping, removed and sent out to be dissected in some lab, where I hoped they'd come to life and eat the faces off of a few pathologists before ultimately getting flushed down a hospital toilet. The icing on the cervical cake was my surgery got scheduled for October 30th. A monstrous tumor being cut out of my body on Devil's Night? Yes, please!

Devil's Night arrived, and while I had initially been told the ovary and fallopian tube would be going along to the internal organ inferno, my doctor changed her tune at my pre-op checkup a week prior to surgery. Although she had spent far longer than she needed to the first time around convincing me that I wouldn't miss the one ovary (seriously, take both of them—I'm a good tipper!) suddenly she wanted to attempt to save the dumb egg-crapping contraption, but wouldn't know if that was possible until the slicing and dicing began. I'm assuming some sort of bonus plan for leaving organs intact had been implemented, thereby creating less medical waste and/or insurance paperwork. You remember Cash For Clunkers? This was Coins For Loins.

So I was left with more questions than answers going into surgery—how long will I be in the operating room, will I be in the hospital overnight, how large of an incision will the procedure require, how many fucking body parts will I wake up missing… all the unknowns were shaken, not stirred, into one giant crap cocktail for an anxiety-plagued control freak such as myself.

While I was deathly scared about surgery, the part that worried me most had nothing to do with pain or whatever parasites might be found leeching from my fertile crescent. I was terrified of going under anesthesia, because once many years earlier I had to be knocked out by medical professionals and I flipped the fuck out, so I was scared I'd lose my shit again. Basically all of my fears boiled down to being afraid of having a panic attack, even though I have them nearly every day anyway. Dumb.

I didn't have to be at the hospital until late morning, which was annoying considering I was scared shitless, extra emphasis on the shitless since I wasn't allowed my morning coffee. I was hoping they would slice me open at six AM so I could have a steamy cup of poop-juice by noontime, but the surgery schedule did not cooperate.

The only thing even remotely interesting from the first two hours in the hospital was having a hose inserted near the crotch of my humongous hospital gown that inflated the whole thing with hot air (or cold, if you prefer your clam slightly chilled), making me look like the Marshmallow Man and that shrunken head dude from Beetlejuice mated and I was their puffy, pan-icky progeny.

Despite my delightfully warm vagina I was still pretty nervous, and becoming more of a raging bitch with each coffeeless minute, but my family didn't seem to notice the subtle difference in my disposition. My mom and my husband had accompanied me, probably just to be sure I didn't run for it. If I hadn't been connected to the twat toaster I might have tried anyway; I was always pretty good at playing Red Rover.

After roughly a thousand hours of lying around being bored, scared, and bored of being scared, the antichrist himself—my anesthesiologist—wandered over to introduce himself. It wasn't easy, but I managed to explain to him that he was my worst nightmare and I thought he should eat shit and die (no offense! *winky face*), and he politely nodded, patted my inflated shoulder, and galloped away on his cloven hooves. I assumed he went to gather the seven horsemen and some virgin blood, or take a pre-procedure piss. Whatever.

Some other scrub-donning jerkoffs then gathered around to unhook my cunt cooker and take some vitals. Then Dr. Demonpants trotted back over, holding a syringe of something green. Our eyes locked and he uttered the words I'd been longing to hear my entire life: "Want me to slip you a mickey?"

I'd never been so smitten.

After my mickey they wheeled me into the operating room and asked me to scooch from the stretcher onto the operating table, which makes me wonder why I even have insurance if I have to move my own ass. My doctor then explained how they would be looking at my innards on the screens hanging from the ceiling all around me, as if I really gave a shit. I could've used some Pink Floyd and maybe a laser light show, but otherwise I was high and happy.

The oxygen mask went on, and it was lights out for Kimmy.

When I awoke in the recovery room the first thing I did was pull up my gown (you're welcome, old dude next to me!) and inspect the damage – three small incisions, one on each side of my lower abdomen, and one puffy cut straight through my belly button, making my naval look like Frankenstein's monster's butthole.

Eventually I was transported to my own little recovery cubicle, where I was reunited with my family and informed that while it was 'tedious work' (I don't know how they code that for insurance, but I'm sure they found a way), in a fantastical feat of operating room heroics the surgeon was able to save my ovary. Like I fucking cared. The doctor, who had promised to save me a teratoma tooth if she found one, described the growth as "large and hairy" but didn't leave me a single souvenir. Other than, you know, some lifelong scars.

Bitch.

I went home later that night, making my exorcism experience – from being dragged in kicking and screaming to being wheeled out drugged and completely chill – about a ten hour ordeal. Not too shabby.

The first few days of recovery sucked. Thanks to a wicked sore throat from the breathing tube, a bitchy bladder, and my beloved anxiety, I didn't get much sleep. The gas they used to inflate my abdomen was not only painful everywhere from my shoulders to my stomach, it also kept me bloated, without the joy of a balmy beaver. Apparently our abdominal cavities aren't quite as easy (or fun) to empty out as a whoopee cushion, which I'm pretty sure drives the final nail into the intelligent design theory's coffin. While I wasn't overly worried about it, six days post-surgery I got the phone call that the pathology report was in, and my hairy little monster was benign. I suppose anytime someone wants to call and tell me I don't have cancer I'm not going to complain.

It's now been over two years, and other than watching my gynecologist eerily admiring my scars and complimenting my "great skin" at our regular preventative maintenance appointments, I've suffered no ill effects.

The strangest part of the whole ordeal (yes, it gets weirder than having a hairy tumor with teeth) was the reaction from others. I mean sure, this fucking thing caused some discomfort and was pretty damn weird, but compared to the multitude of bullshit that going through life being bipolar and with an anxiety disorder has caused, a little abdominal pain wasn't all that big a deal. But with all the flowers, cards, and well wishes, you'd think the toothy little turd had traumatized me for life.

At first I got pissed about the barrage of well wishes that were needlessly pouring in; I've spent my life fighting thoughts and urges that would make even the most gangrenous of growths quiver in their cystic little shells. Nearly every day that I'm forced to go out into the world I face 'fight or flight' panic on level with being attacked by a rabid donkey that's only sustenance has been Viagra enemas. I blow off every obligation I can in order to embrace opportunities to hide from the world, and those breaks only strengthen my fears. I'm constantly being told to cheer up, to calm down, or to just get over it. Then I got a glorified stomachache and suddenly became a target of unsolicited sympathy.

It's amazing (and slightly infuriating) how differently people with "real" ailments are treated. Even my doctors, once hostile,

Ovarian Horror Story

became warm and sympathetic once I was diagnosed with a physical condition. And it was a very minor condition. My recovery time was only a couple of weeks. The recovery time for my mental affliction is NEVER. But if I complain about that I'm just a whiner, or a pill seeker.

Eventually, though, I swallowed my anger, and milked that little lady gremlin for all she was worth. I took the maximum recovery time off of work, and slurped up all the sympathy I could get. Because when you've been told most of your life that you're not actually sick and you just need to suck it up, it's kind of nice to kick back and leave the sucking to everyone else.

Ugly Fuckling

I WAS TOO KLUTZY AS A KID to be labeled a tomboy, but I sure as hell wasn't a pretty little princess, either. It wasn't just my lack of femininity and propensity for vulgarity that precluded me from the tiaras-to-teatime dream castle; I just wasn't cute. In case my big nose and sickly skin tone weren't damning enough, I also walked weird, and mumbled when I spoke. Forget being a princess, I had about as much charisma as a three-legged sewer rat drunk on Drano.

To top it off, I was a skinny little twerp. I was always shunned from sitting on my mom or grandmother's laps, because my butt was too bony. I was practically invisible to boys, and to everyone else for that matter, because when I turned side-ways I pretty much disappeared. Other than one creepy great uncle that repeatedly told me "with eyes like that, you'll be a man-eater" (and he very well may have been referring to cannibalism) it was never assumed that I'd get very far on my looks alone, which was just fine with me.

My point is, I was never vain. I had no reason to be. I may have had a warped and unhealthy self-image, but that was an integral part of my charm.

Kimmy Dee

Maybe that's why I never learned how to use makeup. I didn't figure I'd ever look pretty, so I had no interest in putting in any extra effort. And when all my friends were dying their hair the various colors of the rainbow, I left mine alone. I'm sure that had more to do with my naturally black locks' resistance to color (and fucking light itself), but I also didn't give two shits about altering my appearance to appease anyone, especially myself.

That is until I turned 18, and suddenly got 'hot'. As it turned out, outside of the primarily Dutch blonde haired and blue eyed community I had been unfortunate enough to be born in, my skin tone and hair color weren't actually that off-putting. And you know that mandatory ten pounds that finds its way onto everyone that first year after high school? Well, mine went to my ass. What had once been "too bony" became nothing short of magnificent. So magnificent, in fact, that at the first job I started after high school no one really knew my name; I was just known as 'the girl with the nice ass.'

It turned out that was alright with me, too.

While I didn't know how to handle the attention that suddenly flooded my way, I'd be lying if I said I didn't enjoy it. It's like the story of the ugly duckling; you damn well know that sexy swan strutted its shit everywhere it went, flaunting its feathers, savoring all the stuck up duck bitches' wide-billed stares. She probably blue balled a gander or two as well, just because she could.

But I soon found that with hotness also comes self-consciousness, a commodity I already had in spades when it came to every other aspect of my life. Suddenly, my appearance mattered. And it was right about that time that I began facing down the mortal enemy of emerging arrogance: premature aging.

Gray hair at a ridiculously young age runs in my mom's side of the family. My mom, grandma, and my great grandma, at least from what I'm told, were all nearly completely gray by age 30. I had this fact beaten into my brain from such a young age that, if not already predisposed by genetics, my hair's pigment probably would have given up and killed itself anyway. But I tried to hold out hope that I would inherit the stubborn, color-rich hair of my dad's side. My dad's mom hadn't dyed her hair until she was 50, which, to any 18-year-old basically signifies eternal youth. I mean, who gives a fuck what happens after age 50? By then you're basically dead.

So you can imagine the horror I felt when, at 19, I found my first gray hair.

It wasn't just gray, it was white. White, thick, and wiry. It looked like a pale pipe cleaner twisting its gruesome way out of my skull.

And it wasn't alone.

I felt my newfound hotness disappearing right before my suddenly haggard eyes. My hair was black; I was not equipped to camouflage this nagging symbol of mortality. I never bought into any of that "blondes have more fun" bullshit, but they certainly have an advantage when it comes to not looking like a fucking corpse in the prime of their lives. While my blonde haired, blue eyed nemesis Suzie Slutface was able to pass off a few gray locks as natural highlights, not even twenty-year-old Kimmy Crabass began looking more like Cruella de Vil's uglier (and older) sister.

The eradication of these fossilized follicles became my obsession. Every evening I sat slumped in front of a mirror, fiendishly plucking the ghastly strands from my aging mane. But they only grew back whiter, and thicker. More menacing.

My family, despite being genetically responsible for this curse, wasn't overly sympathetic. I was knocking back my first legal drink on my 21st birthday when my grandma asked when I would finally cut my trademark long tresses, because "no one likes an old lady with long gray hair."

By my mid-20s I would have gone bald if I continued to pull every single ashen-hued hair from my head, so I finally caved and became a slave to the hair dye industry. I would structure my already limited social calendar around my coloring schedule, in hopes of always appearing at my youngest and most vibrant whenever I had to show my stupid face anywhere public. And I still had to yank out a few renegade grays that resisted the dye altogether. The inevitable emergence of even a millimeter of unaltered roots sent me either screaming to the salon or hiding my head in shame.

I could've been the poster child for young women with severely deranged body image issues, except I'd never let anyone put my disgusting mug on display. I refused to be included in group pictures. I avoided looking people in the eyes, for fear that I'd see the recognition of my ugliness reflected right back at me. I wore frumpy clothes, not just for comfort, but to attempt to cover the hideousness that was my abhorrent existence.

And somehow I managed to direct all of this self-loathing toward the pigment-lacking strands of dead cells protruding from my head, mourning the symbolic death of a youth that I hadn't bothered to enjoy.

Some say the only way to truly overcome a phobia is to face it head on, and while I still think sticking your face into a vat of spiders to cure arachnophobia is a bit extreme, there does seem to be some truth to that masochistic parable. I finally managed to find peace with my appearance not by hiding it, but by flaunting it: I became an amateur pin up model.

A friend talked me into doing my first shoot when I was 28. It was a package where you pay a set price in exchange for professional hairstyling, makeup, pose coaching, and photos on a specialized set. Ours happened to take place inside a retro-themed car garage, complete with antique cars to fulfill all of our posing needs, as well as the cars' owners, who were creepily observing the whole thing as they tossed back a few beers and debated the merits of carburetors versus that newfangled fuel injection business.

If you're not familiar, new age pinup is a lot like Glamour Shots were in the 90's, minus the gaudy outfits, obnoxious hair, and hooker makeup. Okay so it's really nothing like Glamour Shots, other than you pay people to make you look and feel like someone special, and both required ridiculous amounts of hairspray.

But there was something exhilarating about being doted on like a movie star. Despite being over a hundred degrees in the garage that day and being watched closely by old men who may or may not have been sporting Cialis-induced boners, my friend and I had more fun than we'd probably ever had sober, which was a state I was really trying to spend more time in by my late 20s. And when the finished photos were sent, I hardly recognized myself – which is exactly what I was hoping for. I looked polished, poised, and maybe even sort of pretty.

And, just like that, I had a new hobby.

While I continued to rock the effortless 'just rolled out of bed and may or may not have even bothered to brush her teeth' look in my daily life (I always did brush, though – teeth brushing and eye crust picking are the foundations of my morning beauty routine), many weekends saw me transformed into an adorned beauty, exuding glamour and grace; that is, as long as I didn't have to walk very far in those six-inch stilettos. You can't cure clumsy, and I was blessed with the natural balance of a premature calf.

I started with photo shoots ranging in style from traditional cheesecake pin up to a geekgasmic Star Trek cosplay. (I wore a red shirt but that's okay, because I have a vagina. It's only the red shirted dudes that are expendable, proving once and for all that there is no room for fuckboys in a utopian universe.) With each shoot my confidence in front of the camera grew, which was not only evident in the photos, but also spilled over into my everyday life. Over the course of a few years my previously nonexistent self-esteem, newly formed out of discarded bobby pins and fake eyelashes, rose to levels almost bordering on healthy.

And the shoots kept getting sexier.

Although I've never actively sought publication for my photos, I did grant permission for one lingerie shot to be included in a magazine. I was probably the only person that purchased the rag, but there's something about seeing your own scantily-clad ass in print that is intoxicating. And, eventually, I quit cladding my ass at all.

My self-esteem goal after I turned 30 was to pose naked, and a few months after that bittersweet birthday I slid off my big girl panties and made it happen. It was a tasteful, rear-view only shot (it *is* my good side) that has only been seen by a few close friends, but I did it—I bared all in front of the camera. And the effect it had on my confidence was staggering.

It made me realize that the human body is beautiful, and mine was no exception. Despite lumps and bumps and protruding bones, I've never been one to judge others on their physical appearances, so why had I always judged myself so harshly? Seeing myself through the lens of a talented photographer, wearing nothing but my own skin, made me realize that my flaws only added to my overall beauty, and I was every bit the woman that the images in magazines had beaten into my brain that I could never, ever be.

From that point forward I held my chin a little higher; which, as it turns out, is a much more flattering position for my big dumb face anyway.

I may have made peace with my body, but I didn't suddenly sprout a big old boner of self-love or anything. There are still a thousand things I would change about my appearance if I could; decades of feeling like a sideshow exhibit don't just melt away in an instant, despite what the latest installment in the Oprah book club might tell you. But I did find acceptance, and learned to appreciate what I have instead of mourning every-thing I lack.

And, honestly, does anyone even give a fuck?

Seriously, shouldn't we have evolved past the whole societal standards of beauty crap by now? I don't care about hoverboards or flying cars, I just want a future where I can log onto Facebook and not see four hundred posts mocking complete strangers because of their weight, hairstyle, or what they wear to do their goddamn grocery shopping. And I firmly believe that being better people has to start with not shaming ourselves. That is, unless it's funny.

By going naked in front of the camera, I became more comfortable being seen fully clothed. While I still rock the unkempt look most of the time, I no longer shy away from the occasional silly selfie, and it's only my debilitating anxiety disorder that keeps me from going out socially, not my fear of having my face seen by the outside world.

Baby steps, people.

And once I started not hating absolutely everything about the way I looked, I became less obsessed with reversing the aging process. I started to stretch out my hair color schedule an extra couple of weeks, and if a social obligation fell the week before fresh color, so be it. I quit plucking the stray grays altogether.

Of course, my outlook on aging didn't change all at once. There was no "A-ha!" moment, where I gave up hair dye and started serving dinner at 4:30 pm so I could be in jammies before Jeopardy came on. And I didn't toss my tweezers, although they tend to get more use around my chin than on top of my head these days. But my childish meltdowns over my maturing features did seem to dissipate with my growing comfort in my own slightly sagging skin.

I'm in my mid-30s now, and the aging process is starting to catch up in new ways. Some fine lines are popping up around my eyes. While I'm still disgustingly thin, I now have some weird pockets of flab I've lovingly dubbed my 'armpit fat'. My once magnificent ass is now sporting a few dimples.

While I don't necessarily embrace these things, I no longer freak out over them, either. Instead I do things that were absolutely unheard of to my pre-30s self – I put actual effort into eating right, sleeping enough, and exercising. I still love doing sexy photo shoots. And while I still can't help but notice my imperfections, I don't dwell on them as much.

I realize that aging isn't always pretty, but it is part of life, and I do prefer it to the alternative. Plus, as a humorist, the natural process of aging provides an endless thread of material.

The other day I glanced in the mirror and saw what I assumed to be an albino cat hair sticking out of my eyebrow. I live with three cats and a dog, so pet hair is basically my glitter. (And also the garnish to my food, which is probably why I don't get many repeat dinner guests.) The offending hair was not only way too long, its color (or lack thereof) was in stark contrast to my dark brows. After casually rubbing at my face a few times and failing to come away with it, I leaned a little closer into the mirror and realized that the damn thing was attached. The mutant whisker was growing right out of my fucking forehead.

The Kimmy of a few years prior would have pulled the demonic fiber from her face, set it on fire, then smashed the mirror so that not a shred of evidence from the alleged follicle debacle would remain. She'd sulk for days, getting out of bed only to stare bleary-eyed at her hideous reflection in the jagged remains of her bathroom vanity, searching tirelessly for more monstrous symbols of mortality protruding disgustingly from her face.

Instead I had a good laugh about the ordeal, my glee only dampened by the fact that I plucked and pitched the strange white strand before I thought to Instagram it. I'm now even considering growing my pubes out, just to see what sort of color show those bitches are capable of putting on.

I'll probably have a few more aging-related freak outs before everything is said and done. I can't say for certain that I won't fall to pieces when I spot my first definitive wrinkle, or the first time I piss myself when I sneeze. But once I shed a few tears, and change into some dry pants, I hope I'm able to laugh every bit as hard as I did at the alien eyebrow... even if the laughter costs me another pair of clean underwear.

Fuck it, especially if it does; what would be better to blog about than a bitchy bladder? The puns practically write themselves.

And you can bet your ass that I'll still be strutting my swan stuff, sporting the sexiest damn incontinence panties money can buy, silvery pubes and all.

Losing Jack

I HAD ALWAYS BEEN A DADDY'S GIRL, but not in the traditional sense. I was no sickeningly sweet, pretty-in-pink little princess, and my dad wasn't a doughy-eyed pushover that believed his baby girl was an angel straight from heaven that could do no wrong. No, my dad and I enjoyed swapping stories of our smartassed antics while we puffed away on cigarettes and jammed out to heavy metal.

Spending Sundays together had been our tradition since my parents separated back when I was six, but once I graduated high school and got an apartment of my own the Sunday visits kind of fell by the wayside. At the time my dad was freshly separated from his second wife, but they still lived together while trying to sort out the logistics of the split, so hanging out at his house wasn't ideal for either of us. My apartment was pretty much a flop house for wayward drunks, so I didn't exactly invite him over to spend time, either. I was freshly free and 18 – my whole life was a blank canvas unfurling before me. I had no idea that my dad's own life was wrapping up for good.

After about a month of tentatively made and then quickly canceled plans, my dad finally pushed me into committing to a lunch date one afternoon before I went to work for the evening. He sounded authoritative about it, which was odd for him in any capacity toward me, let alone in making simple lunch plans. I brushed off his demanding tone as nothing more than stress over his hectic work schedule and failed marriage, but was nonetheless ready and waiting when he arrived at my apartment building to pick me up.

Lunch itself was awkward. When I lit a smoke and my dad didn't, he confessed that he was trying to quit again (he hadn't smoked for close to a decade, but had taken the habit back up a year or so earlier), but he didn't mind that I partook. A couple of times he excused himself from the table to take calls on his cell phone, which was unlike him to do while we were spending time together, but his job as a multi-state representative for a carpenters' union made for many urgent issues to address, and it *was* a Tuesday afternoon. I thought little of it, even if he did seem a little off kilter each time he returned to the table. My dad took his job, and the needs of the impoverished factory workers he represented, to heart. It was nothing for him to receive a frantic call from a floor worker and then jump into his car and drive across three states to face the problem. One worker's grievance was just as important as a thousand to him, so to be visibly troubled by whatever had been said on the other end of that phone wasn't completely out of character. Still, something seemed off.

We ate lunch relatively quietly, but when we got back into his car he confessed his real reason for being so insistent that we see each other: he had been diagnosed with pancreatic cancer.

He had attended a work conference in Las Vegas, and under the desert sun his skin had turned yellow and jaundiced, prompting him upon his return to make his first visit to the doctor in nearly 30 years.

Losing Jack

It turned out all the weight he had been so proud of losing in the previous few months wasn't due to his newfound dedication to dieting and exercise, plus the stress of an impending divorce – he had a large tumor on the head of his pancreas, and it was killing him.

The tumor was located in such a spot that removal was most likely impossible due to its proximity to a major artery, but surgery was going to be attempted anyway, in the medical field's version of the Hail Mary football play. He told me the last call he'd received at the restaurant was the hospital conf-irming that the surgery was now scheduled; he'd go under the knife the following Friday. He asked if I could be there; I managed only to nod my head yes. I was too shocked to speak.

On our way back to the apartment he detoured for a quick drive past the hospital, showing me where I would have to park and such the following week. Despite his diagnosis he was still my dad, and worried about things like his teenage daughter getting lost downtown. He explained that the surgery was complicated and risky, and may very well not be successful. And if it wasn't, well, his odds weren't very good. He didn't elaborate further.

When he pulled up to my door I asked if he wanted to come up, but he said he had to go. He hugged me, and asked if I was okay. Here was a 43-year old man who had just been handed a death sentence, and he was more concerned about everyone else. That was a pattern that would continue for the rest of his life… which wasn't nearly long enough.

I held in my tears until I was safely inside my apartment, but as soon as I crashed through the door I dropped to my knees and cried as violently as I ever had in my life up to that point. I was thankful my roommate wasn't home, because I was not coherent enough to explain myself. My whole body convulsed as I wept. I pounded my fists into the floor, wailing "No, no, no," in between guttural sobs. If my downstairs neighbors had been home they probably would have called the police.

When the flood of emotion finally slowed, when I was once again able to breathe, I did something that would become a trend for me through the course of my dad's illness, and probably long after – I swallowed my pain, and went to fucking work.

***

My mom went with me to the hospital on surgery day. Her and my dad had been amicable with one another most of my life, despite the painful dissolution of their marriage. My mom knew I would need the emotional support, not to mention I was naïve about navigating around the hospital, having been there only a handful of times to visit my grandfather when I was a small child. I cleared her presence with my dad ahead of time, and he seemed relieved that I would have someone to wait with me.

It turned out I had a whole party to wait with.

I was also naïve about the risky nature of the surgery. I couldn't bring myself to accept that it might not be successful. My mind wouldn't even entertain the idea of him not pulling through. But my dad was optimistic. That was another trend that would continue; he would never let on to how dire things actually were. At least, not to me.

But the less callow of my dad's loved ones knew exactly what was at stake.

My sister was away at college and my dad had broken the news to her via phone, and practically forbade her from coming home for the procedure. But my grandma, aunts and uncles, a cousin or two, and even my dad's estranged second wife, Wendy, were there waiting when my mom and I arrived.

That was when the seriousness of the situation started to sink in. I scarcely saw any of my dad's siblings or his mother, unless it was a funeral.

The man of the hour himself was in a room for pre-op, while his fan club gathered in the hallway right outside. My grandma ushered me through the crowd and into the hospital

room, where my dad sat at the edge of the gurney in his hospital gown.

"Nice dress, Pops," I said.

My grandma left us alone in the room. We shot the shit for a few minutes, about everything and anything other than surgery or cancer. Then a nurse came in and announced that she'd be giving him an enema to complete the surgery prep, to which my dad responded with a very Jack-like "Yippee!"

I was ushered back into the hallway, where my mom was staying as far back from the room as possible. She was actually very comfortable with my dad's family. In fact, my grandma and her had continued peddling their crocheted wares at craft shows together, despite the divorce over a decade earlier. But my mom didn't want to make my dad uncomfortable, so she hung back. She was there strictly for me, and didn't want to be in the way. I wanted to cling to her like a toddler, and never let go.

A few minutes of awkward conversation with the family I barely knew passed, then my dad sauntered bow-legged out of the pre-op room – apparently when they give you an enema, they neglect to inform your waiting loved ones that the bathroom is down the hall, and a walk of shame will be forthcoming.

In his infinite humor, my dad, probably clenching his cheeks, danced a little Irish jig in his hospital gown to amuse his waiting fans. Then he hightailed it to the bathroom, where he assured us everything (and more) came out okay.

After the enema business a nurse escorted the family to the surgery waiting room. She explained that we'd be receiving per-iodic updates from the OR, but he was expected to be in surgery for at least eight hours, and no news was good news.

A few minutes later a doctor came in and said two people could accompany my dad back to the surgery holding area, which sounded like a thing for cattle, and he had asked for me and my grandma. Wendy was visibly upset at this, but I paid her little attention as my grandma and I sprung to our feet and were ushered out to be with Jack.

My grandma took one of my dad's hands and I took the other. In that way we flanked the gurney as he was wheeled down to surgery. He was scared. He would never say so, but he was quiet, and his eyes looked like those of a frightened child. I had never seen him that way. It took every ounce of strength I had to hold myself together for him.

The nurses gave us a few minutes alone, just the three of us, and while I can't remember what exactly was said, we were all trying to mask our uneasiness. Eventually my grandma and I were told it was time to go, and Jack hugged his mother first, then me. He held my cheek against his chest for an extra moment, both of us knowing, but neither of us saying, that it could be our last embrace. Then my grandma placed her arm around me, and we walked together back to the waiting room, finally letting the tears win.

***

My grandmother was also my godmother, but I had been excommunicated from the Catholic church when I was seven because my mother was marrying a Protestant, so that title chalked up to a whole lot of jack shit. My dad loved his mother dearly, but he only really took us to visit her on Christmas and maybe a few other short visits a year. So while we weren't close, we had never exactly tried to be, either.

Despite our emotional distance, we held on to each other tightly for that walk back to the surgical waiting room. Once there we separated; my grandma went to sit by her other children, and I was the awkward wedge between my mom and Wendy. And there we waited.

And waited.

I tried to read. I tried to do crosswords. I even tried small talk with the family I barely knew. But the clock wasn't budging.

We watched other families come and go from the waiting room. I was dying for a smoke, but my mom didn't even know that I was a smoker. She had busted me once when I was 14 or 15, but she had no idea the bad recreational habit had evolved into a daily necessity. Or that I chain smoked with my dad for fun. Whenever I said I wanted to take a walk she insisted on joining me, thwarting my nicotine fix. At least my all-consuming craving kept me from agonizing completely over what was going on in that operating room.

A couple of times a staff member did come over to let us know they were still operating, gave a few minute details that didn't really tell us much of shit, and then left us waiting again. Finally, after over eight hours of surgery, an attendant came out and asked that we follow her to a private waiting room.

None of the other families we'd seen come and go had been asked to do this. We all exchanged panicked glances, seeing the fear of the worst spelled out in each other's eyes.

The room was cramped. We were kept waiting for a few minutes that felt like hours, wondering why we were there. The more time that passed, the more sure I became that Jack was dead. They were sitting in the operating room, over his cooling corpse, drawing straws to see which one of the unlucky nurses would have to tell us.

And then the surgeon walked in.

We looked up at him like hungry birds.

"Well, he's in recovery," the surgeon said.

The relief washed over the room. He was alive.

"But we weren't able to remove the tumor," the doctor continued. And just like that, we were suffocating again.

He went on to explain that the tumor was coiled around the artery, and while they were unable to remove it they did remove his gallbladder and reroute a bile duct, for which I'm assuming he had a reason, but it is lost to me now. My guess is they needed some sort of discarded part to bill to the insurance company.

They weren't able to remove it. The surgery was unsuccessful.

My dad was going to die.

They said it would probably be an hour and a half before we were allowed to see him. I had phone calls to make, but the one phone in the room we had been ushered to was in high demand by other family members. Not everyone had cell phones in 2001, myself included. So my mom walked me down the hall to a pay phone.

First, I called my boss. When she answered she almost hung up on me, because I couldn't get my throat to make words. Finally I spit out that it was Kimmy, and my dad was out of surgery but they weren't able to remove the tumor. Then I froze, and hung up. I hoped my boss would assume it was a bad connection.

The next call was to my sister. It should have been the first call, but I needed a practice run.

Jaime better understood the implications of the surgery than me. She was pre-med. She had researched pancreatic cancer, and knew that it had a 2% survival rate over five years. She also knew it would be best to keep that statistic a secret from me for as long as possible.

My mom asked if I wanted her to make the phone call to Jaime, and I said I'd better do it. But once I spit out the words "unsuccessful" I passed the phone to my mom to fill in the meaningless blanks. She hung up after a few minutes, but I was in no hurry to return to the stuffy waiting room, so instead we took to aimlessly pacing the halls of the hospital. A nurse walking towards us veered right toward me, and I jumped.

"Kimmy!" the nurse said.

It took a minute, but I realized the nurse was actually an intern, and my childhood best friend. I had tears streaming down my face and the last thing I wanted was a reunion, so I mumbled "hello" and kept walking. My mom paused a moment to explain my aloofness to the poor girl, but I didn't bother to stop.

We made our way back to our so-called family, and eventually hospital staff came in and told us my dad had been brought to his room and we could come up, although he wasn't awake yet.

We all walked up together, but when we got to the room everyone stopped, unsure of protocol. My mom hung back,

knowing she would not be going inside at all. The rest of us glanced around, and everyone silently pushed me forward, the first one into the room where my dad lay, with tubes coming out of everywhere, hooked to machines that did god knows what.

A nurse was in the room making sure everything was working, and ushered us around. She said he was starting to come to, and we should gather around so that we'd be the first thing he would see when he opened his eyes.

I stepped forward and grabbed my dad's hand, the one that wasn't attached to an IV. It was cool and clammy. Everyone else, save my mother in the hall, gathered behind me. I had been given the lead, whether I liked it or not.

Eventually his eyelids fluttered, and then came to rest halfway open. His hand squeezed mine weakly.

"Were they able to remove it?" he asked. He was hard to understand; his lips were dry and chapped, his throat raw from the breathing tube that had only just been removed.

I couldn't believe delivering this news had been left to me. To *me*. I was barely 18, I knew nothing about anything, and here I was, holding my groggy father's hand, and being asked point blank about the outcome of the surgery, while the "adults" were safely shielded behind me.

"No." My voice cracked, but I didn't drop my gaze from his.

"I didn't think so," he said. Then he closed his eyes and went back to sleep.

***

He slept for a long time and my mom wanted to get going, so Wendy offered to drive me home. Eventually he woke up enough to exchange a few hazy jokes with us, but then visiting hours were over and we were ushered out.

And finally the long, emotional day got some much-needed comedic relief.

Wendy and I walked out with my aunt and uncle, who were parked in the same lot. We exchanged hugs and went our separate ways, which turned out to be only a car length apart. They pulled out just ahead of us, and since it was late the parking attendant had been replaced with a sensor-operated drop-down gate.

My uncle pulled up and the gate raised, allowing him to drive underneath. Wendy, in her haste, tried to follow him through, but the gate dropped down and bounced with a thud three or four times off the roof of her car. We erupted into some much-needed laughter, and, for a moment, it seemed everything would be okay.

It had to be.

***

As a second shifter and also a teenager, I typically slept late. But the following morning I was up before the sun.

Prior to my dad's surgery I had bought a couple of books to help him bide the time during recovery. We both loved reading, and it was all I could think of (or afford) to get for him. I hadn't brought them on surgery day, however, because I knew he wouldn't be clearheaded enough to pay attention to them. But I wanted to be there the moment visiting hours started that day to present my gifts.

I did manage to be the first visitor that morning, and my dad rewarded me with an extremely weak, "What the hell are you doing here?" as a greeting.

"Where else would I be?" I said.

I gave him the books, and he thanked me. I tried to ask him about his condition, but he avoided the questions. Instead he turned it to my latest predicament, which was never ending car trouble. I was still driving my very first car, the one he had bought me when I turned 16, and it was giving me a lot of problems. Knowing that he wasn't going to be able to work on it for me anymore, he suggested that I go out and look for a replacement. I was working full time and able to

afford a small car payment, so he starting giving me pointers. I wasn't a total moron when it came to vehicles, but he knew that any car lot would try to take advantage of an 18-year-old girl. He suggested I browse lots that were closed on the weekend, to avoid being hassled.

My dad, who had just been cut open from one end to the other and given a death sentence anyway, was telling me to leave his bedside to go shopping.

Soon my grandma arrived and asked if I wanted a hamburger, and we went to the hospital cafeteria for lunch while my dad napped.

When we returned to the room he was sleeping, so I honored his wishes and left to go look at cars. I returned later that evening, at which point he told me he'd be released in a couple of days and would be staying at my grandma's, and to just come visit then. I left reluctantly, unable to shake the idea that he just did not want me there. He didn't want me to know what the doctors were saying. He tried like hell to protect me from the severity of his prognosis, beginning to end, and this turned out to be barely the beginning.

When I pulled up to my grandma's house a few days later in my new-to-me car, I found my freshly discharged dad lying on his back on the kitchen floor, reapplying trim to the edge of a countertop, despite his stem-to-stern incision.

"Want a hamburger, Kimmy?" my grandma asked. It was always a hamburger. I nodded yes. She seemed happy to have purpose, and set the frying pan on the stove.

My dad rose gingerly, asked if I wanted to sit outside. It was a beautiful spring day. I nodded.

I asked what came next, and my dad said once he was healed enough from surgery he would start chemo and radiation treatments. The doctor had advised him that such treatments were rarely successful with his type of cancer and may only reduce his quality of life for whatever remained for him, but he wasn't ready to give up. He said he had too much life left to live, and that he would beat this.

I believed him.

My grandma came out of the house with my hamburger at about the same time Wendy pulled into the driveway. My dad excused himself, bathroom emergencies becoming a quite common occurrence, and I was left to gum at my cheeseburger while Wendy spun to me her sad tale of an abandoned wife.

She was upset that my dad had chosen to recover at his mother's instead of at home. She wanted to take care of him. She wanted *him*. But he had told her to "stop acting like a wife", and that nothing had changed between them. I felt for her; I knew my dad's words could sting. I also knew he wasn't the type to mince words, and if whatever had transpired between them had been enough to sever their relationship when he was healthy, he wasn't going to relent while sick. I began to wish she would just go away, and eventually she did.

Jack liked my new car.

***

Knowing it was past time to part ways with Wendy once and for all, my dad decided to move to Indianapolis. Considering his work area consisted of five states, his new home would be more centrally located. He asked if I had any friends that could help him pack up the U-Haul on the Michigan side, as he was still under lifting restrictions from surgery, so I recruited a couple of guys from work and we handled it.

Not wanting to go through the hassle of finding a new team of doctors, he made the five hour trip back to Grand Rapids for his appointments. He had a port surgically implanted into his chest for chemo, so instead of having to sit in a chair while the poison slowly dripped into his bloodstream through an IV, he was being constantly dosed as he went about his days. He joked that it was his USB port, and that he should be able to plug in and charge his laptop between shots of chemo. As for radiation, he realized quickly that he wasn't

able to plan other activities on those days, as the treatments made him violently ill.

We started getting together for lunch more often than we had when he was presumably healthy and living in the same city. He downplayed the severity of his sickness, constantly joking about 'radioactive diarrhea' and the doctors insisting so hard that he must be feeling abdominal pain from the tumor that they did everything in their power to make sure his gut felt miserable. But I could see that he was growing shaky, and even more distressing were his eyes; there was no fire there at all.

Of course I said nothing, and didn't push him for details about his prognosis. I was barely an adult; I had no idea how to process anything that was going on, let alone offer support.

After our biweekly lunch dates I would cry into a pillow for a few minutes, then get up, clean myself up, and go to work.

***

Everything is as it should be.

A few weeks before his cancer diagnosis, my dad was driving somewhere in Columbus, Ohio, when he heard those words.

"Everything is as it should be." He said later that the voice was as clear as if it was coming through the car's speakers. He was so mesmerized by it that he drove a complete loop around the city.

He had never been an overly religious man. He was raised Catholic, and often joked that he took pills to cure him of the condition. In the last few weeks of his life he did seek comfort through faith, as so many terminal patients do, but prior to that he didn't really speak of his beliefs, of lack thereof. At least, not to me.

But even in full health he took this guiding voice, whoever or whatever it was, as a spiritual experience. At the time, he thought it was referring to some conflict he was facing in his work, and he was being divinely reassured that he was on the right path. But when his grim diagnosis came right on the heels of this bizarre occurrence, he came to see it as a symbol of comfort and hope.

***

Chemo and radiation treatments continued for a few months, and while they made him sick, they were working. The tumor was shrinking.

In fact, by the time he finished the scheduled treatments, the tumor was undetectable. His doctor didn't want him to get his hopes up, but all signs pointed to the cancer being in remission.

He told me this over one of our lunch dates. It was all I could do to not jump for joy right there in the restaurant. While he passed on the disclaimer that his doctor had given him, that the cancer may come back in full force now that treatments had ceased, his eyes shone with the life they had been lacking. He was actually beating this!

The checkups continued every few weeks for a couple of months, and all of them came back clean. Finally, about seven months after he was told he had three to six months left to live, it appeared he was cancer free.

And, for a little while, it felt like everything really was as it should be.

***

My dad called one afternoon and said he needed to talk to me about something. My heart dropped; my stomach lurched. The tears pressed against my lower eyelids; a quiver of my lip was all it would take for the levy to burst.

False alarm.

He was wondering if I'd be willing or able to find a way to take in one of his dogs. When he split with Wendy she kept two and rehomed the other two, but one of them – my

dad's absolute favorite four-legged creature on Earth – wasn't working out in his new home. With his traveling, it simply wasn't possible for him to keep a dog. But he knew that this dog and I shared a special bond; the dog would just hear my name and go bonkers. The dog knew me as Kimberly… making Gibby and my dad the only two beings on the planet that refused to shorten my name.

Gibby was a sheltie that my dad had bought Wendy for her birthday the first year they were married. I had been eight years old. Although he was Wendy's dog, he took to my dad right away, and vice versa. He was the most intelligent dog I've ever known, yet couldn't quite grasp that he didn't have to bark his face off every time the door opened or closed. Whenever I visited, though, he was *my* dog. He was my sidekick, and I had missed him terribly. We joked during the phone call about whether Gibby would show preference to my dad when he visited, the way he clung to me when I was the guest.

I told him to give me a few weeks, but Gibby would have a home with me.

The apartment I was living in didn't allow dogs. After some searching and penny scraping I found a place that would allow Gibby, as well as the two cats I already had. The rent was more than I could afford, but I'd figure it out, even if I had to take on a second job. Which is exactly what I did. I picked up a part time gig as a gas station attendant, adding 30 hours there to the 40 I was working as a second shifter at a car dealership.

And the first time my dad was in town and visited us, his face lit up brighter than I had ever seen when Gibby smothered him in doggy kisses. I managed to hold back the tears, because even the happy ones are for sissies.

And after Gibby got done mauling my dad, the little bastard was back at my side, proving once and for all whose dog he really was.

Kimmy Dee

***

Something really strange happened over the next few months. Both my dad and I found love.

He became serious with Angela, a coworker that he had a cross-country billiards feud boiling with. Since their jobs kept them out on the road, they'd often connect at the end of the day, to see where one another had ended up. Then they'd each drive however many hours it took to meet in the middle, at the nearest pool hall.

She was from bumfuck Indiana, but her southern drawl screamed Kentucky or Tennessee. She was over a decade younger, and a computer nerd back before everyone on the planet was a computer nerd. She was small, sweet, and absolutely fearless.

I found my match in Andy, a coworker at the car dealership. I had been having a string of bad luck in the love department, and swore off trying to find a boyfriend in favor of just having some fun. Andy was six years older than me, and relatively new to town. It wasn't long before we realized we shared a lot of the same interests: music, playing cards, and mass consumption of mind altering substances.

He invited me over one night for a card game with his roommates, and from that evening forward we were inseparable. The irony of swearing off love only to be broadsided by it wasn't lost on me.

That Christmas was my merriest ever.

My dad and Angela came into town, and so did my sister. We had never met Angela; my dad had not met Andy. Yet the five of us, along with Gibby, exchanged a few small gifts and a whole lot of laughs in the cramped dining room of my second floor apartment. I was 19, and it seemed that being an adult was going to be just fine.

More than once that night we could all be heard repeating the phrase: "Everything is as it should be."

***

A couple of months later Jack complained of an ulcer.

He mentioned it a couple of times when we chatted via phone or email, which meant he had to have been hurting pretty badly. He didn't ever want to worry me, so he always sugarcoated the extent of his suffering, which would later lead to a pile up of kid-guilt that I'll never be able to outgrow. But for now, it was just an ulcer.

Or so he thought.

Angela had moved into his apartment in Indianapolis with him, and together they made the five-hour trip to Grand Rapids to see his doctor. It was both a routine checkup and a consult regarding the so-called ulcer.

I had known they were coming up, although I don't believe we had planned to get together. But I received a frenzied phone call from Angela that afternoon right before I went to work; my dad was being admitted to the hospital immediately. The doctor suspected the worst.

I told her I'd call in sick and head right over, but she said there wasn't anything I could do, and they wouldn't know anything until they were settled in anyway. So I brushed myself off, went to work, and waited.

I worked as a service writer, which is not at all as creative as it sounds. Basically if your car broke I was the person you'd be stuck talking to about it. Mechanics often aren't the greatest at dealing with people, plus their time is valuable, so service writers act as translators between the customer and the technician. It's certainly not the most stimulating job on the planet, but since everyone I interacted with was sure to be in a bad mood it was often stressful.

I worked second shift, 3:30 to midnight. I typically walked in to a melee that tapered off about six or seven o'clock, leaving my evenings open for some chain smoking and solitaire. But those first few hours were always a bitch.

And it was during those hours that I was staring at the phone, waiting to hear what the fuck was going on with my dad who, until a few short hours ago, was by all accounts considered a walking miracle.

Finally a call came in, from my dad himself. He was settled into a hospital room, and in the morning would undergo his second major abdominal surgery. A scan had showed something large blocking his stomach. His "annoying ulcer" had actually kept him from keeping any food down for over a week, a fact he'd glossed over in our previous conversations. His doctor suspected it was a new tumor. Or several of them. They had to open him up to find out.

I made arrangements to take the following day off from work, and arrived at the hospital many hours ahead of the scheduled surgery. This time I came alone, being much more adept than I'd ever wanted to be at navigating through that hellish hospital.

Jack was propped up in his hospital bed, barking orders into his cell phone. Angela greeted me with a smile and warm hug. When my dad hung up I asked if he ever took a day off, and Angela confided that the call was for her. Since they had come into town anticipating only a day trip she didn't pack replacement contact lenses, and was blind as a bat without them. My dad made his most urgent matter of business before being sliced open (and possibly given his second death sentence in a year) getting an optometrist to transfer her prescription so she could pick up some lenses locally. I'd like to say he was just trying to distract himself, but he really was simply that damn concerned.

I got to spend some time with just the two of them in the room. My dad was on a morphine drip that he'd push a button for when he was feeling pain, and every time he did he'd smile at Angela and whisper "white rabbit." They were both so calm. And so in love. The happiest damn couple, despite impending tragedy. I couldn't help but smile with them, even though it felt like my heart was being ripped from my chest as the surgery hour ticked closer and closer. He was

going into surgery cancer free, and would potentially come out a lost cause. Yet here we were, having fun.

He eventually drew an audience of my grandma and maybe an aunt or two, but not nearly the fanfare that the first surgery had brought in. I was glad for that. And with Angela there, I didn't feel as trapped. She was practically blind, but instead of sitting in the waiting room for hours on end the two of us ventured around the hospital, her hanging onto my shirt for guidance. Mostly, though, we sat outside, smoked cigarettes, and talked about the world crumbling around us. I became closer to her in that day than I had ever felt to anyone.

A few hours later, back in the waiting room, the surgeon called us together. I couldn't help but notice that we hadn't been shuttled off to a private room.

It wasn't cancer.

It wasn't cancer.

The blockage in his stomach was simply built up scar tissue, a byproduct of all the radiation treatments. They rerouted some things, fixed his plumbing, and in a few days he'd be released back to his life. His *cancer free* life.

They don't allow champagne in the hospital, but our celeb-ration wasn't any more subdued because of a lack of alcohol. It was cheers, happy tears, and thankful prayers all around.

When my dad opened his eyes this time, he saw Angela first. And he could see in her eyes that everything was as it should be.

***

With Angela, my dad truly made Indianapolis his home. He found a local doctor he liked, and his day trips to Grand Rapids became fewer and further between. I stayed busy working the two jobs, as well as building my life with Andy. I still talked to Jack nearly every evening via email, and it seemed everything was going just fine. As it should be.

It wasn't.

He hadn't told me he'd been getting sick again. Or that he was growing weaker every day. Or that he had gone to his new doctor to have these things checked out.

So when I called to wish him a happy 45th birthday on July 2nd, 2002, I was caught completely off guard when he told me he'd just found out the cancer was back. It was in his liver.

I tried to mask my shock at the news by saying something about that diagnosis being a pretty lame birthday present, and he responded with a casual, "Well, it's a birthday I wasn't

supposed to have."

His optimism was both awe-inspiring and contagious, and I didn't doubt for a minute that he would beat cancer for the second time. I didn't even cry at the news.

Six days later he called to let me know that he and Angela had gone to a small chapel outside of town and gotten married.

He'd never sounded happier.

***

A few weeks passed, then I received a concerned phone call from Angela.

She was worried about Jack, and wondered if I could come down for a visit. Although I emailed back and forth with my dad nearly every day, asking him point blank how his treatments were going, it turned out there was a lot he wasn't telling me. Apparently he rarely felt well enough to even leave the house. She hoped a visit from me might lift his spirits a little.

That weekend Andy and I made our first road trip to Indianapolis.

My dad called at one point when we were on the way down, and seemed disappointed that we were still a few hours away. I was a teenager as well as a second shifter, so getting up and moving on a Saturday morning wasn't really

my specialty. It seemed odd that he was so antsy, and I instantly felt guilty for not getting up at the ass crack of dawn and hitting the road.

When we arrived at my dad's apartment Angela was out doing some shopping. He made a joke of giving us the grand tour, but he moved slow and seemed a bit weak. Despite being a sunny day, all the curtains were closed and no lights were on inside. The living room, kitchen, and one bathroom were located on the main floor, and upstairs were two bedrooms, one of which was fashioned into a home office, as well as another bathroom. The apartment was easily twice the size of mine, and his rent was cheaper. I made a mental note to consider moving to Indy.

After the tour, which lasted about ten minutes, my dad settled back into his recliner in the living room and suggested that Andy and I head down to the apartment complex's rec center and check out the pool. He was feeling a little tired, but Angela would be home soon and they were going to take us out that night.

We obliged his subtle request to be left alone, despite it being inconsistent with his impatience for us to arrive.

Neither of us were too keen on swimming, and I hadn't really developed an affinity for sunbathing yet. I was still a recovering goth, after all. I wasn't wearing all black anymore, but I still valued my pasty complexion. (It was hard work to keep my olive skin from tanning, but I managed. I was a creature of the night, and all that.) Mostly we poked around the fitness center and shot the shit about everything but my dad's frail state.

We killed about an hour and a half before heading back to the apartment. Angela had made it home, and the atmosphere inside had brightened considerably. She asked if we'd all be up to going to a movie, which was apparently exactly what my dad wanted to do, so we loaded up and went to the nearest theatre to see what was playing. This was new to me, as my dad and I had always checked show times and planned our day accordingly, but Angela was more spontaneous, and we opted to just decide what to see when we got there. We ended up watching Men in Black II. It was terrible, but in that funny way.

Afterwards we headed back to the apartment, and since it was a beautiful night we sat outside on the patio. My dad had a couple of beers in the refrigerator left over from someone that had visited, and asked me to drink them for him. I obliged.

The four of us sat outside talking, laughing, and swapping stories until three in the morning. Often Jack would just sit back and listen, always smiling.

Angela told me the next morning that it was the best day he'd had in a long time. It was mine, too.

We all hugged goodbye and Andy and I headed back to Michigan victorious. We had elevated my dad's mood, gotten him out of his funk… everything was as it should be.

***

A month or two later my dad was involved in a car accident.

It was his fault; he ran a red light and slammed into another car, totaling his vehicle in the process. No one was hurt, thankfully, but when the cops arrived my dad was so incoherent they thought he was either drunk or on some seriously heavy drugs. He was slurring terribly, and couldn't tell them where he lived or even who he was.

Eventually, somehow, they got enough information from him to get a hold of Angela.

Apparently he had been on his way to a meeting with his boss, something she had begged him not to attend, as he had been weak and having cognition problems, and was angry about situations at work that had his head clouded enough already.

She got him home, where he slept for nearly an entire day. While he slept she got a hold of his doctor, who said this might be it; he very well could be dying now.

When he woke up he was completely normal, and the whole experience was chalked up to a weird reaction to his medications.

***

As summer made way to fall my work schedule was running me down. I was getting sick a lot, my roommate and I weren't getting along because of my spending every moment with Andy, and something had to change. It didn't take long to realize it was much cheaper to own a home than to rent, being pre-housing bubble America, and with Andy I felt confident enough in our relationship to plant some roots. So, a few days before I turned 20, I signed the closing papers and we moved into our very first house.

My dad was happy for us, and not the least bit concerned about his youngest daughter's decision to live in sin. He was a little wary of the neighborhood where I had settled, but even before the leniency in lending caused a catastrophic housing crisis a teenager making eleven dollars an hour couldn't afford to be too selective.

I was able to quit my second job, but I stayed pretty busy with working one full time job, caring for Gibby and my two cats, trying to make our new house feel like a home, and drinking myself stupid. I may have been a mostly responsible kid, but I was still a kid. Not that I ever really outgrew the drinking habit, but at least I had an excuse back then.

I still talked to my dad through email almost every day, but we never really discussed plans for us to make another visit. He remained vague about his condition, and I didn't pry. I assumed we had time, and he didn't give me any indication that we didn't.

So it came as a bit of a shock when he told me in early November that his chemo and radiation treatments had been put on hold indefinitely. He was no longer well enough to tolerate them, according to his doctor. He scoffed at the situation, acting as though it was only a temporary setback. I was too naïve about matters of life and death to know any better. I could have, and should have, done my own research. No one lived and died by Google back then yet, but information was still easily available. But at that age I wore rose colored glasses, and everything was as it should be, and a doctor pulling the plug on the only trusted treatments for a terminal illness wasn't the end of the world. My dad said he was fine, so he was. He had beaten it before; this would be no different.

I did finally mention that I'd like to visit soon, but he said that they had decided to make the trip up to Grand Rapids over Thanksgiving. He wanted to see my grandma, and to see my new house, so we should just wait the couple of weeks and we'd see each other then.

During those weeks of waiting we continued to communicate as normal. I'd ask how he was feeling, he'd say fine. My sister would be in town for Thanksgiving as well, and we were excited to be all together again for the first time since that perfect Christmas. I counted down the days.

When the holiday finally arrived, we tentatively planned for my dad and Angela to come over Thanksgiving evening. I always celebrated the annual feast at my grandparents' house on my mom's side, and my dad was spending the day with his mom and siblings. Andy and I rushed out after eating so we could do some last minute cleaning around the house, but my dad called a little after we got home and said he was very tired from traveling and visiting with family, so they had checked into their motel for the evening. I had to work on Friday night, so they'd just come over on Saturday.

I was a little bummed that I'd bleached out the litter box for nothing, but they'd be in town all weekend, so no rush. If I had known what was coming, I may very well have begged them not to come at all.

***

Saturday morning preparations around the house consisted of hiding the bong, cleaning up the freshest splatterings of Gibby

vomit, and noticing something I had neglected to clean every-where I looked. I wasn't used to entertaining guests, and hadn't really developed good housekeeping skills yet. I alternated peeking out the window and frantically dusting things, until finally I saw my dad's car creep up and park across the street.

I turned from the window and stashed the cleaning supplies I had scattered all over the kitchen, and tried to get in some last-ditch tidying. I was so worked up over the cleanliness of my house that I gave little thought to the fact that I hadn't seen my father in four months, the longest I had ever gone without seeing him in my entire life. That fact was about to sock me hard in the chest, and the accompanying mindfuck would prove to be permanent.

I put the cleaners away and took a few calming breaths, surprised that there hadn't been a knock on the door yet. I went again to the window.

Angela was out of the car, and had come around to the driver's side, which was the side closest to me. She opened the door, and a stranger rose slowly from the driver's seat. He was tall like my dad, but rail-thin, barely half as wide at the shoulders. He took short steps, his long, bony legs making it seem like he was walking on stilts. As they got closer I could see his skin was gray, and waxy with age. His hair was thin and limp, and his cheeks so sunken it seemed that I was staring right through to his skull.

I couldn't breathe. My stomach twisted and my head went dizzy. I wanted to run away. I wanted them to turn around and leave. I didn't know how I could open the door to this… creature. This apparition, which was hobbling toward the front door of my house, its steps supported by the loving arms of my father's wife.

I swallowed hard with my hand on the doorknob. I took one last stinging, jerky gasp for air, and slowly opened the door.

My legs weakened as the pair shuffled into the entryway, and it took every ounce of concentration I could muster to not drop to the floor. The room was spinning. My whole life was spinning, as I found myself looking into the yellowed eyes of the decrepit being before me.

I exhaled, all rational thought and childhood naivety escaping with the breath from my burning lungs. This was real. The being before me was no ghost, he was my father. And he was dying.

I closed my eyes tightly and threw my arms around him. I could feel his shoulder blades sharply protruding from his back. Where I would once bury my face in his arm I felt only bone. I feared that my hug would hurt him. My dad, who stood 6'3" and weighed 285 pounds while at the peak of his health, felt as though he might crumble in my arms. Still we held each other for what felt like an hour, but I doubt either of us was strong enough to hold ourselves standing for more than a few minutes. I was surprised that either of us could stand at all.

"Hi Dad," I whispered without breaking the hug.

It wasn't emotion that held me close to this Jack-like creature, though; I held on only because I was terrified to meet its eyes again.

***

I spent the rest of that day trying not to look at my dad without it becoming obvious that I couldn't handle seeing him. We made him comfortable (or as much so as he could be, considering) in Andy's recliner in the living room, and we spent the day playing with Gibby, watching movies, and straining to make small talk. It seemed stupid to talk about anything other than his condition, but I don't think I could have handled a conversation about that if anyone had started one. So we pretended that four months hadn't imposed forty years' worth of wear on him while instead marveling at the dog's good health, despite his own advancing age.

Jack did seem to be in good spirits, though, as he chattered on to Angela about his favorite spots in his hometown. He probably knew he wouldn't make it back again. We talked

mostly about bars and restaurants, and he decided he wanted to go out to one his favorite places that was a combination of both.

While the last thing I wanted to do was go out, you don't argue with a dying man when he says he wants a wet burrito, so off we went to Lenny's.

The place was absolutely dead, which was probably for the best. We weren't a very lively table either, as none of us were drinking (if I had been of legal age I would've downed enough booze to drown a horse), and the seating arrangements had me sitting right across from him, so there was nowhere else to look.

After eating, Jack excused himself to the restroom. With him finally out of earshot I tried to talk to Angela about his condition, but a shitty band had started playing to an audience of none and drowned out any chance of conversation. All I managed to glean from her was that she hadn't really noticed the drastic physical changes in him because she was with him every day, and that he never gave me the full truth of his prognosis because he wanted to protect me from it. After that everything faded into tuneless, distorted noise.

Unable to talk, we all just stared at each other for what felt like an eternity. I wondered if we should send Andy into the men's room to check on Jack. The minutes kept on ticking, the only one not seeming overly concerned being Angela. When I was finally able to gesture to her that I was worried, she said it always takes him a while, he was okay.

Sure enough, about twenty minutes after excusing himself, my dad hobbled back to the table. Seeing him walk up had nearly the same effect on me as it had earlier in the day. He didn't feel like he could sit back down on the hard chairs, which seemed like the perfect excuse to get the fuck out of there.

We went our separate ways after that, as my dad was tired and ready to go back to their motel for the night. They would be headed back to Indy the following day, but were meeting my grandma, aunts, and uncles for brunch first, and asked if we'd tag along. I agreed, even though the last thing I wanted to do was relive this horror again the next day. We exchanged nerv-ous hugs in the parking lot, and then Andy and I headed home.

I had never been happier to get away from my father.

***

I was exhausted, mentally and emotionally, but I didn't sleep much that night or for many nights after. Every time I closed my eyes I saw my dad's frail frame and sunken cheeks. And those yellow eyes, which had once been big and brown like my own. I could still see him when I opened my eyes, and I recoiled with fear. I had become a child having nightmares of the boogey man, except this boogey man was real, and he was my father.

Guilt over being so appalled by my dad's appearance combined with the dread of seeing him again the next morning, and I had never hated myself more. The man was dying, and I couldn't even bear to look at him. My emotions were twisted so tight that I spent hours shaking with nervous anguish, a sort of throbbing despair that was only made worse by knowing the coming daylight wouldn't solve a goddamn thing.

I tossed and turned until morning, when we finally got up and headed out to meet the whole damn family at the trashiest food trough in town.

I had never been to an Old Country Buffet, and it didn't turn out to be quite the shitshow of society that I had been taught to expect. Or I was just too caught up with trying not to scream to notice my surroundings. Regardless, the only thing that truly horrified me about the place was that I was so caught up in the shock of my dad's appearance to be of any use to anyone.

The rest of the family, however, didn't seem to have the same hang up. For never having been close, they sure got along well. And they absolutely adored Angela. We all did.

I can't imagine what those months would have been like without her.

The restaurant was part of a small, barely used mall, and after we ate a few of us walked around a little. There was a corner that was roped off with yellow "do not cross" tape for no apparent reason, so logically we all stepped over it and posed for a family photo. Afterwards my dad and two brothers "assumed the position" with their hands against the wall, and someone snapped a picture just as my dad moved one of his hands to grab Uncle Jim's ass. I've come across those pictures a few times in the years since; I still can't bring myself to look at him. And that fact still fills me with shame.

We said our goodbyes in the parking lot for the second day in a row, but this time my dad and Angela were heading back to Indy. I hugged them both tightly, despite my fear, and held in my tears. I didn't deserve to let them fall.

***

I was a mess the rest of that day, and when night rolled around I told Andy I couldn't go to bed. I knew it would be like the night before; that I'd see him every time I closed my eyes. I needed a distraction. He didn't try to talk sense into me. Instead he gathered up every single blanket and sleeping bag we owned, and made a giant "bed" on the floor of the living room in front of the TV. And that's where we slept every night for many months to come.

***

After his oncologist had halted treatment my dad began seeking out clinical trials to get involved in. He wasn't ready to give up. Every experimental treatment he applied for he was disqualified from because he was either too sick, or not sick enough.

One particular possibility had him meeting with a physician in Chicago. The doctor deemed him ineligible for the trial, but was optimistic that he could still help him. Despite planning only for a daytrip, and even having food in the crockpot back in Indy, my dad was admitted to the hospital that afternoon. Angela drove all the way back to Indianapolis to turn off the crockpot (and grab contact lenses), then right back to Chicago to be at his side.

Of course this all happened on a Thursday, so he ended up being doomed to the hospital bed for the weekend with no news. I was going to drive down, as Chicago is only half the distance of Indy, but at the last minute my dad called and begged me not to come. He didn't want me venturing out alone. Despite being packed and ready to head out the door, I honored his wishes and stayed put.

On Monday they released him from the hospital; the doctor had concluded there was nothing they could do.

***

Jack hadn't been working much, and not at all outside of his home office, but at one point during the latter part of his illness a major rally was taking place in the heart of his constituency. He not only made it there, he got onstage and delivered a rousing speech.

I was working that evening when Angela called. I panicked; we always emailed, a call could only mean bad news.

Instead, she was giddy. She said my dad had been a hit on stage, and his very presence inspired masses of workers in a way that was nothing short of magical, and the two of them were too excited to keep it to themselves.

She handed my dad the phone, and while he didn't say much, I could hear him smiling. Everything was as it should be.

***

My guilt over being afraid of my dad's appearance was only overshadowed by my guilt for having not seen him for so long. During our emails after the Chicago incident I got him to agree to be more forthcoming with me, however unpleasant the information. We also arranged for Andy and me to visit, just two weeks after that horrible Thanksgiving weekend.

The road trip this time, and every time after, was filled with dread. I was so scared to see my dad, to see how much worse he might look since the last time, that I spent the entire five hours just a notch below hyperventilating. It would be a few years before I'd be diagnosed with an anxiety disorder, but I think those months gave me one hell of an introduction.

While still a shock initially, I did grow more comfortable with my dad's appearance. It pained me to see how he was suffering, but I got to the point where it no longer scared me. I still was not prepared to think of a world without him, though, and knew that eventually he'd be accepted to a trial that would lead to a cure. He'd have to get better. Because everything was as it should be.

The four of us sat in the living room and talked of old times, and while it was lacking the optimistic magic of that evening in July, it was good to be together. My dad grew nostalgic, and while unable to move much from his recliner, he directed me on where to find a home video he still had of a homerun he'd hit in a softball game when I was a kid. The ball had sailed over the fence and smashed into the windshield of a car passing by on the road beyond. Someone had caught it on tape, and I watched his face as he watched his younger self on the TV. He looked a hundred years old, but with a child's gleam in his eyes.

Angela had excused herself while I was digging through videos, and she reemerged and sat with me on the couch. She held out two necklaces and asked which one I liked best.

Both had green gemstones hanging from silver chains. I looked carefully at both, and pointed to the one where the stone was in the shape of a heart.

She handed me the chain, and said, "Take it. It's yours."

"Really?" I said.

"Yes. It's jade, it's always meant good luck to my family."

I put the necklace on, and Angela headed back upstairs with the other piece of jewelry. I looked over at my dad and, while I never in my life saw him cry, his eyes were misty. He told me that the necklace I was wearing meant a lot to Angela, and that he was incredibly happy that she and I had become so close.

Since that night I have worn that necklace on days when I felt I needed some extra strength. Over a decade after my dad passed I visited my grandma, Jack's mother, at her deathbed. She was barely conscious, but having fits of anxiety. I placed the necklace in her hand, closed her fist around it, and whispered to her that what she was holding represented Jack. Although she wasn't communicative, her grasp tightened. I left the necklace with her that night, and she was still holding it over 30 hours later when she took her last breath. My uncle returned it to me at her funeral, and a few months later I was wearing it when we said our final goodbyes to my dad's sister. I don't know that the necklace has been good luck, but it has been a source of comfort, which I now know is sometimes the same thing.

***

Andy worked every other Saturday, so we decided we would make the trip to Indy every two weeks. The ride down was always the same – colon-clenching fits of anxiety and dread over seeing my dad two weeks closer to death; mid-mortem, though I was far from accepting that as an inevitable fact.

Each time he looked worse. Each time his body grew weaker. But we were together. And we watched shitty movies and told stupid stories, and when I got home I'd snuggle up to Andy

on our blanket bed on the living room floor, and then I'd plod my way through two more weeks of work.

Then the visions started.

They were daydreams, really. Two of them. They haunted me. In the first I saw my dad stumbling on those shaky legs, then falling. He wasn't strong enough to get up, and I was unable to help him. Even in his sickly state he was a large man, and I couldn't lift him up. And the absolute worst part of the vision was the look of hopelessness in his eyes; the embar-rassment, the despair at having become nothing but a nuisance. My dad was a big, strong guy; taking his strength from him was as bad as taking his life.

In the second vision I received a phone call. He was dying. I jumped in my car and high tailed it for Indianapolis. Every time, I didn't make it. I was always somewhere in Indiana when I got the phone call that I was too late. He was gone, I was alone, and in the middle of fucking nowhere.

Those two visions played like a goddamn loop in my brain. While I worked, while I fitfully slept; they were all I saw. They became my obsession.

I confided them to Angela, as her and I began talking much more regularly. My dad was getting too weak to spend much time on the computer, and his hearing had always been shit when it came to phone calls, so my daily communications began coming from her.

Christmas crept up on us once again. My sister had a break from medical school, and while we had always celebrated Christmas Day with my dad as kids, his mom and siblings were going down for the actual day so we decided that the three of us would go the weekend after.

To call that holiday bittersweet would be an understatement.

Angela had gone bonkers with gifts. They'd gotten me an automatic cleaning cat litter box and a top of the line coffee maker, the latter of which made my mornings better for over a decade. I knew they spent a lot more money on us than they could afford; even the best insurance crapped out once your medical expenses more than quadrupled your income.

But the best gift of all was a Hallmark-type book titled *Why a Daughter Needs a Dad*. While cheesy on its own, my dad had gone through it page by page and made handwritten notes. Most of them were cute reminders that men were scum, but on the last page he wrote, "And dads need daughters like Kimberly."

***

Our Christmas visit was a day longer, and before we left the final day my dad wanted to go out to eat. He hadn't left the apartment in weeks. We went to Ponderosa, which was his choice, but I was a bit leery of taking him to a buffet since he was so shaky on his legs.

It was a disaster. We helped to get him whatever he wanted, but once he got out in the late December cold he could not get warm again. We wrapped him in all of our coats, and still he sat at the table trembling. He couldn't eat, he just shivered. He was 45 years old, but looked at least 90. He was embarrassed by the attention and wanted us all to eat and carry on, but each of us would've given anything in the world just to warm him up.

Andy had packed our car before we went to eat, so when we returned home and got dad inside we said our goodbyes and hit the road.

My sister and I chatted a bit on the way back to Michigan, mostly her feeding me facts I wasn't ready to face. She told me he was not only dying, he was close. I refused to accept it. Her medical training aside, he had beaten it before and he'd beat it again.

We dropped my sister off and headed home, where we crawled into our blanket bed and turned on the TV.

I awoke to an email from Angela. Shortly after we'd left the night before my dad had fallen. She hadn't been able to help him up. He laid on the floor and cried until she ran to the next apartment, where she'd found a kind neighbor to help. Nightmares really did come true.

***

Shortly after Christmas my dad was placed under Hospice care.

I didn't really know what that meant, other than he would be receiving medical care in his home, and I clung to my optimism for his eventual recovery. Because a daughter needs a dad, and everything is as it should be, and someday this would be nothing but an unpleasant memory.

Angela relayed to me a couple of days later that the Hospice nurse had told her he probably had two to six weeks left, and in his advanced stage of sickness he was especially prone to bouts of dementia, and could even turn violent against those caring for him. She said already he had gone through a couple of incidents where he awoke screaming because he thought he was inside of whatever show happened to be on television when he fell asleep.

I was getting ready for work when she dropped these bombs on me, and I crumbled. I tried to sop up the tears with tissues as they fell, but they were flowing too fast. I had never been the praying type, but I did pray that day.

I turned my tear-streaked face toward the mildewed ceiling of my shitty house, and through clenched teeth prayed, *"God, if you're going to take him from us, then please just fucking take him."*

***

We stopped at a run-down shack of a restaurant on our way out for our next bi-weekly visit. I wanted to surprise my dad with a burrito from his favorite place. The burrito made the ride to Indy in the frozen trunk of the car, while I shivered in the front seat for reasons that had fuck-all to do with the temperature.

Jack was now completely confined to the upstairs of the apartment; he could no longer make it up or down the stairs.

So instead of hanging out in the living room, he was sitting in the office he shared with Angela. They each had a large computer desk that sat facing opposite walls. She had gotten him one of those long metal grabbers because he couldn't stand up to grab anything, and when they were in the office together he would use it to reach over to her desk and raid her candy dish. Despite everything, he managed to find a little fun.

Climbing the stairs to see him that day, however, felt like scaling Everest. On top of my usual dread of seeing how bad he looked, I had the added fear of not knowing if he'd even know who I was, or even worse, if he'd act out violently. I was terrified.

He looked tiny in his high-backed office chair. With his leathery, wrinkled, discolored skin, he reminded me of the shrunken heads associated with voodoo and witch doctors, only the effect covered his entire body. He was mostly just a sack of bones, except his lower abdomen was painfully bloated, making it look like he was wearing a bulky fanny pack. Every few days the hospice nurse would stick a needle into him to drain off some of the fluid to provide some short-lived relief. His feet were so swollen that he couldn't fit them into size 15 shoes, which were the largest you could buy in most stores; he had been a size 13 before getting sick.

He joked that he was bummed that he wouldn't be able to go out dancing for a while.

While I had once been unable to look him in the eye, now they were the only part of him I could stand to look at. I could still see *him* in them. A tiny pinpoint of light buried deep behind the yellowed and dulled irises, where my real father could peek out of the dungeon that was his failing body, and when I looked at him directly in that spot I could feel his thoughts and all of his pain, and I would have traded places with him if I could have. He knew he was beat. And even worse, he felt guilty for it.

Sensing we were having a moment, Angela invited Andy to go with her to rent some movies. But the interruption broke

the spell, and soon I was sitting in a chair next to Jack's while we scraped the bottom of the small talk barrel.

The conversation turned to football, and that was when I noticed hints of dementia for the first time. It wasn't anything important; just mixing up teams, using baseball terms, talking about scenarios that hadn't happened as though they were memories. While it was trivial shit he was getting goofed up about, I couldn't help but think back to the warning of possible violence, and I got scared. As I nodded along with his nonsense I kept wondering what I would do if he tried to harm me. Would he lure me to him for a hug, then try to strangle me? Would I even fight back, or just let my nightmare play itself out? And why did I keep returning to this place of fear, when all the dying man really wanted was the unconditional love of his daughter?

I was saved by the bell, as the pizza delivery arrived before Angela and Andy were back. While I ran downstairs to pay and take care of the food my dad stumbled to the bathroom. He didn't make it out of there until after Angela and Andy returned, cutting our dad and daughter bonding time short. At the time I was thankful for that. Looking back, not taking advantage of that time to talk candidly with him about life, death, love, and everything in between is one of my most persistent regrets.

***

We piled into the bedroom to eat pizza and watch the crappy movies Angela and Andy had chosen. Hospice had set up a hospital bed next to my dad and Angela's king size pillow fortress, as their bed was far too tall for him to get in and out of anymore. We got him situated, and then the three of us got cozy together in the big bed.

I never did get truly comfortable, though. The volume of the television, in order for my dad to hear it, was deafening to me. The room smelled like sickness. While the hospital bed was so close to the regular bed it was almost touching, it felt a world away. I tried to imagine how isolated he must feel, confined to a fraction of his apartment, lying in what he knew would become his death bed, while the people he cared about more than anything in the world ate pizza and popcorn and carried on like the world wasn't ending.

We stayed this way through three agonizingly long films. Each moment I felt like my insides were being twisted, and it took all I had to not run screaming from the room, from the apartment, getting as far away as my legs would carry me before the frigid January air mercifully froze the air in my lungs and put me out of my misery. Instead I sat in the bed and wrung my hands until the final credits of the final movie rolled, counting the seconds until Andy and I could safely retire to the downstairs sofa bed.

***

I was the first one up in the morning, and was having coffee at the dining room table when Angela came downstairs. She told me my dad was awake, and would love it if I went up and had my coffee by him. It was the absolute last thing I wanted to do, but after stalling for a few minutes I went up.

He was lying in his hospital bed watching a Sunday pregame show. A couple of NFL playoff games would be on later. I joined him and we chatted a little about the scheduled games, but not much else. He seemed more coherent than the previous evening, but also more down.

We were leaving that afternoon, so with the five hour drive ahead of us we couldn't stay real late. My dad was bummed; our visits were always so short, with arriving on Saturday afternoon and leaving 24 hours later. I told him I'd try to take a vacation day at the end of the following week, so our next visit could be longer.

While we watched football Angela did some cleaning, and Andy went to work doing things around the apartment – assembling a few things, some minor repairs. Jack's gratitude to him was a little disproportionate – you'd think Andy had

performed open heart surgery, not put together a drying rack. But it turned out my dad was thankful to Andy for more than just taking care of the chores he no longer could. Angela later told me that when he was first diagnosed he worried the most about me, which even *he* thought odd, as I had always been the "strong" one. But now that I had Andy, he knew I'd be cared for. And he knew Angela would be okay, because she had me.

Everything was as it should be.

It got to be time to go, and despite how uncomfortable being there always made me, I didn't want to leave. Jack had never left the hospital bed that day, other than a couple of shaky trips to the bathroom. Andy gave him a handshake, at which point my dad thanked him again for helping around the apartment, and then he headed downstairs to load the car.

I walked over to the hospital bed and took my dad's hand, looking deep into his eyes, to that small spot where he still lived. Then, without knowing why, I dropped to my knees, wrapped my arms around him, and placed my head gently upon his fragile chest. He hugged me back, and for an unmeasurable amount of time we just held each other silently. If I close my eyes now I can still feel that embrace.

I was the one to finally break it. I pulled my face up to his, kissed him on the cheek, and told him I loved him. I got to my feet and headed out, turning back when I reached the doorway of his bedroom to wave and blow him a kiss.

That was the last time I saw him alive.

***

The following weekend my sister and her boyfriend were planning to make the trip to Indy. Angela had updated me throughout the week on my dad's worsening condition. The dementia episodes were getting worse, and he wasn't getting out of bed anymore except to use the bathroom. The couple of emails I got from him were jumbled and senseless. Angela tried to set up a web cam so we could talk, but it didn't work.

I offered to come down for the weekend again, but Angela worried that it would be too overwhelming for him having both me and Jaime there, so to keep my plans of coming down for a three-day visit the following weekend. I put in a request for the vacation day, and it was approved.

It ended up being the day of his funeral.

Jaime called from my dad's on Sunday morning. They had gotten there the previous afternoon, and it had been the visit from hell. On Saturday evening my dad fell off of the toilet, and Jaime's boyfriend had to help Angela get him back to his bed. If Stephen hadn't been there to help, who knows what she would have done.

Sunday morning, my dad started screaming.

"*He has Jaime, and he has a gun!*" he was yelling. Angela, trying to calm him down, explained that Jaime was in the kitchen. She was fine. My dad wouldn't believe her. He was adamant that she was in danger.

Angela brought Jaime to him, showing him that she was safe.

"*Where's Kimberly?*" After finally accepting that Jaime was not in danger, his fears became directed toward me.

They tried to tell him that I was at home in Michigan, that I was fine, but he wouldn't calm down. Eventually he dozed into a fitful sleep.

Jaime was crying on the phone. I couldn't believe it; in a week his mind had deteriorated so much. She said they had planned to stay until Monday afternoon, but were going back early.

"He doesn't even know we're here," she said.

Before they left, Angela went to the store and bought adult diapers so there wouldn't be another bathroom fall. She told me that upon seeing them, instead of making a Jack-like joke, he simply wept.

***

I was driving. Angela rode shotgun. Jack sat in the middle of the cramped backseat, flanked on each side by my grandma, aunts, and uncle.

I pulled into a big empty parking lot. It was the type of lot that would normally be adjacent to a large store, like Walmart or Target, except there were no businesses in sight. Just empty parking spaces, as far as the eye could see. I drove to the very edge and parked. Ours was the only car around. I looked back at my dad and he nodded, so I threw the gear shift into park, and we all piled out.

Everyone stretched their legs. I have no idea how long we'd been driving, but it felt like forever. Except my dad wasn't standing there with us. He had gotten out of the car and walked over to the grass that started where the asphalt stopped, and just kept going.

I jogged to catch up with him. Everyone else stayed back. He kept walking until the way was blocked with a chain link fence that spanned from one horizon to the other. On the other side, more grass. The long, flowing grass of a hilly meadow, the greenest I had ever seen.

He looped his fingers through the fence and tried to climb it, but he was too weak. He kept trying, growing more and more frustrated each time he was unable to make his failing body do what he wanted it to do.

I noticed that the fence had come detached from the poles near the bottom. I reached down and lifted the meshed metal nearly to my waist. My dad smiled, ducked, and walked underneath the fence. He never looked back; he just kept walking. I watched his back get smaller and smaller before disappearing completely over the first knoll. I felt both elated and hollow as I stood there, on the parking lot side of the fence, and turned to see the others still by the car, watching and smiling.

I woke up and looked at the clock next to our makeshift bed on the living room floor: 7:02 AM.

***

Being a second shifter I didn't have to be up until one in the afternoon, and usually stretched my sleeps close to that mark. After my dream I fell back asleep and slept hard, harder than I had in months. When I awoke for good at noon, I had a voicemail from Angela. It simply said to please call her as soon as possible.

I dialed her number as I rubbed the crust out of my eyes.

"Kimmy," she said. "Your dad slipped into a coma about seven o'clock this morning."

***

My mind numb, I got myself dressed and headed to work. My heart was screaming that I needed to turn my car south and go to him, but one of my dismal premonitions had already come true, and the situation was out of my hands now. The hospice nurse had come and said it could be hours or days; there was no way to know for sure.

It was a cold Monday in January. Martin Luther King Jr Day.

I walked into the typical craziness at work. It was an endless stream of customers, on the phone and in person, from the moment I walked in the door. I was finishing with one with a line of others waiting when my cell phone rang, followed immediately by my direct work line, and then my cell phone again. The customer rolled her eyes; no doubt she was cond-emning me as unprofessional, having all those personal inter-ruptions. I rushed her off and then, as opposed to waving the next one over, I grabbed my cell phone as it was ringing for around the tenth time.

"Hello?" I said, turning away from the line of grumbling customers.

"His suffering is over," Angela said. I could hear her tears. It was barely five o'clock. If I'd left when I'd found out about the coma, I'd have been somewhere in the middle of Indiana.

I stumbled out into the shop to get away from the customers. I grabbed onto the work shirt of the first mechanic I saw, who was also a dear friend, and hid my body behind him.

"My dad just died."

***

There is a lot more that could be said. That night I traveled back to Indy, where I stayed until the day after the funeral. The emotions of that week alone could fill a novel. But this piece was meant to be about Jack, and on January 20th, 2003, at the age of 45, his story concluded.

I received one last gift from him. He had ordered Jaime and me identical bracelets for Christmas, but they had arrived a couple of weeks late. My sister had gotten hers on that hellish final visit, but I didn't receive mine until after he was gone. Angela handed it to me after we finalized the funeral arrangements the morning after his death.

Engraved on the bracelet was the famous Ralph Waldo Emerson quote: "What lies behind us and what lies before us are tiny matters compared to what lies within us."

Finding Pat

I'VE ALWAYS WANTED TO TRAVEL, but thanks to my bank account balance (plus that whole crippling anxiety disorder thing) I don't venture beyond the Midwest a whole lot. Hell, I barely even leave the house. I mean, I'd love to see the world and all, but the inside of a barf bag looks pretty much the same everywhere on Earth, so why should I spend my hard earned cat food money on airfare?

And I don't do any better on road trips. Riding as a passenger in a car is an almost guaranteed panic attack trigger for me. But since driving a car isn't exactly a foolproof panic deterrent, very few people will climb into a vehicle with me in the driver's seat. I can't say I blame them, really, but I drove my mom and daughter over a thousand miles for a beach vacation in South Carolina and only had a panic attack and got the minivan airborne once the entire trip; meanwhile my in-state 'I'm on probation but I'm going to go on vacation anyway goddamnit' road tour, where my husband drove every mile, was riddled with more palpitations and hyperventilating than that coked out Chris Farley "Chippendales" audition. But I can't blame my potential passengers; having a panic attack behind the wheel is a terrifying experience, and I'm glad I've never had to watch the doom unfold secondhand.

Despite all this, I recently flew 2300 miles before riding shotgun for another 1200 in a booze-fueled pilgrimage to spread my late father's ashes, and check off a few bucket list items along the way.

My dad had requested that his ashes be spread at his favorite place on the planet – a canyon in Palm Springs, California, where he had proposed to Angela. Their mutual lucky number was thirteen. The thirteenth anniversary of his death found her finally moving on with her life and living in Portland, Oregon, and my only real travel desire being to see and hug the redwood trees of northern California, so we decided I'd fly into Portland and we'd make the drive together down to Palm Springs, groping a tree or two in between.

And thus I embarked on a dizzying one week tour of the Pacific Northwest, Southern California, the desert, and the depths of human despair.

As expected, hilarity ensued.

I was nervous to fly, but I did find comfort in the fact that I was at least traveling alone for that portion of the journey. My anxiety is usually amplified when I'm surrounded by loved ones; I can grit my teeth and get through nearly anything on my own, but throw a concerned friend or family member into the mix and I turn into a helpless, panicky puddle. I'm sure Dr. Freud would have a theory about that, but unless he has a solution he can kindly go fuck himself. Or his mother, as he was a bit obsessive about that. Anyway, it was nice to be flying solo.

My local airport is called Gerald R. Ford International, probably because the name implies that, despite its grandiose title, it is mediocre at best. To get pretty much anywhere that isn't Florida you have to take one of those rinky-dink shuttle planes into a major hub, generally Minneapolis, Chicago, or Detroit. My dad had always called those little turds of the sky 'puddle jumpers', since they generally were used only to turbulently skim over a Great Lake or two, and joked that instead of a runway they took off via a slingshot. This memory did not ease my apprehension about boarding my first flight,

Minneapolis or bust. Especially since the "bust" ultimatum left us plummeting to our deaths into the icy waters of Lake Michigan. Or worse, making a successful emergency landing somewhere in Wisconsin. However, the most agonizing part of that short flight ended up being small talk with the sleazebag seated next to me, and before I could blow my complimentary in-air rape whistle we had touched down onto the frozen tarmac of Minneapolis-St Paul.

Although my layover in the Gopher State was a short one, that didn't deter the airport staff from having a little fun with us Portland-bound passengers by switching up our departure gate three different times. And each time the terminal screen updated with the new information, my fellow travelers and I would roll our eyes as we gathered up our Starbucks and shimmied our scrawny legs in an anti-rhythmic attempt to shove our giant iPhones into the tiny pockets of our skinny jeans as we shuffled off in a disorganized flock; just another herd of nomadic hipsters bound for the homeland, not stopping to sojourn until we hit the next complimentary USB charging station.

Once the little game of musical departure gates was completed (all to the tune of some indie band you've probably never heard of), I had little to fear about my flight into Portland. Seated right in front of me on the plane was a large bald man with a giant cross tattoo on the back of his neck, so I knew God wouldn't let anything happen to us.

Just a few short hours later, I was on the ground in Portland.

And, an agonizing handful of minutes after touching down, my bladder made my historic visit to the Beaver State official.

My dad always said "You have to pee there to be there," and truer words regarding domestic travel have never been spoken. This is why I always up my coffee-drinking game as I approach a state line, because visiting a new territory doesn't count if your urine doesn't have an opportunity to sully the groundwater. And if that blessed man with the Jesus ink had taken any fucking longer to collect his carry on from the overhead storage bin, I would have been claiming his shoes as my latest travel conquest. But since God was on his side, and I devoutly do my kegels, I was safely squatted in the first stall of the airport terminal's ladies' room when my levy finally let loose.

And with the fanfare one comes to expect from the enthusiastic (and often premature) automatic flushing of an airport toilet, it became official: I had arrived in Oregon.

***

Angela scooped me up at the airport and we met Mike, her husband, for lunch. It had the potential to be seriously uncomfortable, meeting my dead father's wife's new husband (and staying a couple of nights in his home), but when he started mocking me about my Midwestern roots the moment after we said hello I could tell we were going to become fast friends. You see, true smartasses not only appreciate one other, we also tend to form solid bonds based around our uncanny ability to incessantly belittle each other.

He was my kind of people.

After lunch Angela dropped me off at her house for a quick time zone adjustment nap while she wrapped up her work day. I managed to completely adjust my internal clock to Pacific Time with one half hour power nap. (However, upon my return it took four weeks, a couple hundred cups of coffee, bucket loads of pharmaceuticals, and a demon-summoning séance or two before I was able to respond to my dreaded Eastern Standard alarm clock with anything but a sledgehammer.)

That evening the three of us took the train downtown so that I could experience Portland.

The first thing I learned about the Pacific Northwest is that the people are generally incredibly polite, which I got my first distrustful taste of while using the public transit system. We Midwestern folk like to think that we have the market cornered on neighborliness, but Portland showed me that we're really just a bunch of pharisaical pricks. And the

unsettling phenomenon of people not being complete dicks all the time wasn't confined just to Portland; everyone I encountered on my entire trip was suspiciously pleasant.

People out west have these strange little sayings, such as *"Excuse me!"* and *"Go ahead, you were here first."* I was just getting used to being smiled at by strangers without instinctively grabbing for my pepper spray when, on the last night before returning home, fate finally dealt us a rude waiter. Sensing he couldn't possibly be local, Angela asked him where he was from. His smug reply: Michigan.

Figures.

Daily transit passes are purchased on the honor system: there is nowhere to scan, swipe, stamp, or otherwise prove you put some cash into the station's kiosk. You just board whenever, exit at whichever stop feels right, and if someone ever actually stopped to check if you have a ticket they'd probably apologize to you for the inconvenience. We don't even do charity on the honor system in Michigan; if I give my expired can goods to the homeless I want a receipt, goddamnit.

When someone projectile vomits on a train in Portland, not only does the puker personally apologize to all of the other passengers, the city evacuates that train car until a full and thorough cleaning can take place. Meanwhile, the Detroit People Mover's track is lubricated primarily with human feces, and if someone pukes we just throw a handful of road salt over top of it and curse at anyone holding up the line because they're scared of getting a little stomach splatter on their shoes.

It was also on the train that I discovered there's a road in Portland named Couch, but it's not pronounced couch, like the piece of furniture you sit on in your living room. No, it's cooch, as in the slang term for a vagina. While this little nugget of Portlandian vernacular became a fun little running joke between the three of us for the duration of the trip, it totally stuck with me, so for weeks after I yelled at my dog to quit jumping on my *cooch* with his muddy paws.

Once we got downtown Mike and Angela treated me to a whirlwind tour of Portland's most important places. I was skeptical when they demanded I eat from one of the bazillion food carts permanently stationed there, having a "once bitten, twice shy" relationship with street food (it was a hotdog stand on Water Street in Milwaukee and I'm still sorting through it with my therapist), but, as the saying goes, "When in Rome, eat chicken shawarma fresh off a glorified gut truck." Needless to say my expectations weren't high, and my oft-irritable bowels shuddered a nervous tremble.

After ordering, the vendor prepared the sandwich right in front of us. Well, in front of Mike. I had wandered off to stare at a neon bar sign shaped like an evil cheeseburger. I still had doubts, but in a few short minutes I had in my hands probably the freshest, most mouthwateringly delicious pita-wrapped sandwich I'd ever eaten. And not so much as an annoyed rumble was felt from my intestinal jungle.

We enjoyed our walking tour of Portland under mostly clear skies, just a few sprinkles every now and again. Compared to the icy wasteland from whence I had fled that very morning, the weather seemed quite pleasant. So when we were preparing for some Oregon and Washington sightseeing the next morning and Mike asked if I had packed a raincoat, I laughed in his silly Northwestern face.

You see, we have no use for such an item in Michigan. Of course it rains there, but for six months of the year the rainwater is frozen when it falls to the ground, and the bitterly cold air makes your face hurt. Rainy days are our nice days, and only a sissy would need special attire for such conditions. We had snow suits and ski jackets; for rain you wore shorts and a t-shirt with the sleeves cut off. To make matters more dumb, when he asked it was perfectly sunny outside.

And just like that the sky instantly went gray; the heavens opened, and down poured the fury of a thousand disgruntled gods. Within minutes everything within sight was flooded, and the water kept falling at a rate of four arks per hour.

"Welcome to Portland," Angela said. "I'll grab you a raincoat."

***

We had a great day gazing at spectacular waterfalls while getting drenched by the torrential drizzle of Pacific Northwest winter, the combination making it especially strange that when, after crossing the Bridge of the Gods into Washington State, I developed a little performance anxiety when it came to peeing there to be there.

But a handful of drinks and a few bites of food later I was finally ready, and after sending an in-action selfie to each of my waiting admirers, I was greeted with a standing ovation as I returned victorious, having officially made the Pac-NW my bladder's bitch.

And with that it was back to Portland to get drunk, for the next morning Angela and I were headed to California, the ashes of my father in tow.

***

We called him Pat.

My dad's name was Jack, but for the three days that his Earthly remains traveled in a Ziploc bag inside of a backpack nestled in the trunk of a car, he was Pat.

Apparently there are strict laws regarding the transport of human remains, even after they've been reduced to nothing but dry calcium phosphates: basically, a bag of bone dirt. Angela had been given a certificate by the crematorium to keep her legal when she picked up the decorative urn which contained all that was left of my father, but thirteen years and multiple cross-country moves had left that little piece of paper lost somewhere in the shuffle. However, Mike had been elected caretaker of a recently departed relative's ashes, and her certificate was conveniently close at hand. Her name had been Patricia.

So, as far as anyone outside of the car was concerned, we were traveling with Pat.

Every time we said the name it reminded me of the recurring androgynous Saturday Night Live skit, which had been one of my dad's favorites. I have no doubt that he would have appreciated his (or her) new moniker.

It seemed silly to me to even worry about the legalities of traveling with what looked like a bag of powdered clay, but Angela was adamant that California was notorious for its random roadside 'check points', and the last thing we wanted was to have my father confiscated, his final resting place becoming the inside of an evidence locker in some bullshit municipality cop shop. It turned out that she was right about the check points, as we were stopped a couple of times and asked if we were harboring any firewood or fresh produce not purchased in the Golden State, but not even once were we asked if we were transporting any human remains. It seemed Pat had dodged that proverbial bullet; had we brought along any lemons or lumber, however, we probably all would've been headed to lock up.

The road stops were short, sweet, and relatively harmless, but still they seemed incredibly foreign to me. I can't imagine such an inconvenience ever being tolerated in Michigan. I mean, we have laws about transporting firewood too; we're not savages. But stopping every single car for a potential search, even if the occupants are white? Ted Nugent's head would pop up from the hatch of his recreational M1A1 so fast that his obnoxious facial gestures and belligerent right-wing buzz words would cause the Mackinac Bridge to crumble from all the stupidity. (By the way, Portlanders – it's pronounced Mack-ih-*NAW*, and we'll kick you in the *cooch* if we ever catch you saying Mack-ih-*NACK*.)

The roadside commie-stops weren't the only part of California I struggled to wrap my cute little Midwestern brain around. At our first Golden State gas stop Angela asked me to get out and do the pumping; she'd been spoiled by the mandatory full service Oregon gas stations, and since I've never lived such a hash pipe dream, she figured I'd finally start to pull my weight by becoming the official gas pump bitch.

I hopped out of the Cadillac (did I mention we were driving the coastline in a Caddy?), swiped my card, and lefty-loosied the gas cap. Everything was going smashingly until I removed the pump nozzle, and, well, it had a foreskin.

I'm not one to judge on appearances, but I've only ever been with gas pumps that were more, you know, aesthetically pleasing. I wasn't sure exactly what to even do with this hooded beast. It didn't seem to fit right, and I wasn't sure if I should hold the extra piece up and out of the way while I did what I came to do. It was very uncomfortable for everyone involved.

Much like its penile counterpart, I learned later that the gas nozzle foreskin's purpose isn't really clear, and no one agrees on whether the nozzle operates better with or without it. But, at least for the gas pump, the illusion is some sort of emissions-friendly vapor lock, which seemed all fine and dandy once I figured out how to affix the nozzle to the filler neck (and I was never really sure it was all the way in), at least until I tried to set the trigger lock to keep that sweet petrol stream flowing, and there wasn't one.

At that point I was certain I had entered a third world country, because inhibiting the free flow of gasoline is a mortal sin near the Motor City. You see, "going green" hasn't really caught on in the Midwest quite yet. Hybrid vehicles are a rare sight, but if you do see one there's a good chance that it's in a ditch, having been laughed off the road by a giant SUV with a decorative nutsack dangling from its trailer hitch, towing an overweight trailer full of additional gas-guzzling toys. Be it snowmobiles, speedboats, four wheelers, or dirt bikes, we have a damn fun reason to rape the Earth every season, and the idea of having to stand there and keep the gasoline nozzle depressed with our own hands (or hand; it really only takes one) is an infringement of our God given right to go take a piss while the Earth's blood gushes into our Humvee.

We drove through torrential rain in Oregon and into Northern California, but the mild temperatures at least saved us from having to try to figure out how to put chains on our tires to make it through the mountainous pass along the border. Mike had sent us equipped with chains and the link to a helpful YouTube video explaining what the hell we were supposed to do with the damn things, as a couple of weeks before the area had been hit with major snow. While I'm sure it would have been hilarious if we had to chain up, I'm equally sure we would have plummeted to our deaths off the side of a mountain… which also would've been pretty funny.

Shortly after crossing into California and declaring that we were carrying no unlawful firewood or produce, it happened: I saw my first redwood trees.

I had worried that finally seeing the redwoods wouldn't live up to my expectations. I had been yearning to feel tiny next to these ancient marvels my entire life, and too often experiences that are placed on such pedestals end up being disappointments. Anal sex and superhero movies come to mind. But it turned out my fear was unwarranted.

We pulled off the road just inside the forest, the canopy of the trees providing some shelter from the rain, and walked among the giants. My anxiety over being a road trip passenger, amplified by a killer hangover, melted away as I surrounded myself with nature's majesty. I was gearing up to choose which lucky tree I was going to attempt to wrap my arms around in my ceremonial redwood inaugural hug, when Angela interrupted my reverie.

"These aren't even the big ones," she said, as she motioned me back to the car.

I picked my jaw up off the forest floor and hopped back in the Caddy. We drove through a few more miles of forest, and soon we reached our first checkpoint, as well as another major milestone for me on my whirlwind tour of the west – Crescent City, California, and my first glimpse of the Pacific Ocean.

Finding Pat

***

Since I had never seen the Pacific Ocean, plus was dying to spend some time among the redwoods, Angela had booked an oceanfront room at an inn in Crescent City where she and Mike had once stayed. It was a relatively short first day of traveling, with only about 330 miles clocked, but bought us some great views, as well as a great starting point to explore the forests the next morning.

I felt a little flutter when I laid eyes on the Pacific for the first time, but that may have just been gas from the greasy road food I had shoved into my face hole to appease my hangover. It was incredible to be gazing upon the largest body of water on Earth and all, but the sheer size of the thing is beyond comprehension when you're looking at just a tiny little milli-fraction of its coastal boundary. Having lived my entire life in the Great Lakes region, seeing water that seems to stretch on forever in each direction isn't exactly a novelty. But my inner geography geek finally overpowered my cynical nature, and I was giddy by the time I was able to hop out of the car and stand close enough to taste the spray as the boundless gray waves crashed combatively against the breakwater. About thirty seconds later, however, my giddy ass realized it was struggling way too hard to stand its ground against the winter wind, and we decided to do the rest of our ocean gazing for the day from the comfort of our hotel room, with pajamas on our butts and drinks in our hands.

Our room was perfect: third floor, ocean side, two king size beds, and a balcony we managed to stand on for almost fifteen whole minutes, snapping pictures of the strangely peaceful January sunset without getting too devastating a windburn.

Angela had packed a couple bottles of wine, but being a girl of class, I wanted a goddamn beer. There was a full service bar at the hotel, but we wanted to shut out the world and get cozy in our room. The little sundry store in the lobby had a walk in cooler with a small selection of six packs, so I selected the only brand represented that didn't remind me of redneck piss, and after paying roughly twelve times the suggested retail price I was back in the room, jammies on, and ready to crack open a cold one.

And I nearly busted open my hand.

In my haste to not drink recycled urine, I had neglected to notice that my upscale beers were also not equipped with twist-off tops. Normally that would be fine and dandy, as I have bottle openers stashed in every drawer of my home, but not a single one had made it into my luggage.

Angela giggled into her wine as I trudged down to the bar, in my pj's, and asked the bartender if she had a spare bottle opener. I got the snotty look I was expecting, which was eerily reminiscent of the face I made at the Coors just a few minutes before in the walk-in cooler. She shook her head "no", but out of the kindness of her heart (and to get me to go away so she could go back to smugly perusing her magazine) she popped the top on my beer, and I went back to the room at least sort of victorious.

We sprawled out on our beds and enjoyed our beverages and our view, and despite sipping slowly it wasn't long before my bottle was empty, and I was thirsty for just one more. But the very last thing I wanted to do was leave the comfortable room, especially to go crawling back to the patronizing protector of the sacred bottle opener in the hotel bar, so I did the only logical thing: I whined as annoyingly as possible, in hopes that a better solution would present itself.

And it did, with Angela performing a magic trick of the MacGyver variety.

Sick of my bellyaching, she grabbed a fresh beer out of the refrigerator and glanced around the room.

"It's all about leverage," she said, sounding more like a physics professor than a wine-sipping transporter of fraudulent human remains.

After picking up, examining, and then discarding a few objects, she finally settled on her hairbrush. She flipped the brush around, lodged the blunt edge under the beer cap, and in one beautiful motion she brought her brush hand down, and just like that there was the unmistakable pop that always precedes drinking time, and the newly freed cap pinged across the room.

"Leverage," she repeated as she handed me the beer.

And with that, any doubt I may have been harboring about whether my dad had chosen the perfect woman to spend the rest of his way too short life with flew away like a freshly liberated beer cap.

I carried those other four overpriced beers with me for the rest of the trip, finally drinking the last one on my last day in California. All four times I asked Angela to teach me the hair brush trick, but I never quite got it.

It's good to have friends with leverage.

***

We awoke early and ate breakfast in the hotel restaurant. The day started sunny, and the ocean that had been gray and threatening the evening before was now a deep turquoise with a light blue haze hanging above the water line. The waves continued to spray over the rocks, but lacked their previous fury. The Pacific was at peace, and I couldn't imagine a better way to wake up for a long day of traveling.

We set out on the famous U.S. Highway 101 that hugs the coastline, with the sun shining on our faces and Pat secured in the back, every mile bringing him closer to being returned to the Earth.

Around every bend was a stunning new view of the ocean, and we stopped often to take pictures and to just stare, trying to take it all in.

Soon the ocean views dissipated, and we were back in the forest.

Despite having nearly 600 miles to cover that day, we were in no hurry. This leg of the trip was the reason I flew into Portland to begin with, as opposed to just meeting up in southern California. Because I had suffered some of that dreaded passenger seat panic the day before Angela let me drive for a bit, but we soon realized there was simply too much to see, so she switched me back. She had made this trip before, and I probably terrified her with my distracted gawking.

Multiple scenic routes crisscrossed the 101, and we detoured onto nearly all of them. Some were flooded, the area having suffered seriously heavy rainfall and mudslides in recent weeks. At one point we took a wrong turn toward a scenic overlook and ended up driving two miles over a washed out two-track running along the side of a cliff before the trail was wide enough that we could turn around. We saw an "End the Water Crisis" sign, which I assumed was advertising preservation, poking out of a flooded field. We watched wild elk graze on the side of the road. I spotted the redwood I wanted to hug, and Angela slammed on the brakes to make it happen. We walked a quiet forest trail. I hung out of the moon roof and took video as we cruised down the Avenue of the Giants. Through all of this, we scarcely encountered other humans. I had tall expectations for this tiny section of Earth, and the experience managed to shatter them all.

As the afternoon crept on we found ourselves headed out of the forest and into wine country, and once again we were driving through torrential rain. It was as though the redwoods had been my fair weathered wonderland, but now the dream was over, and it was still wintertime in northern California.

Finding Pat

The ending of my dad's all-time favorite poem, "Stopping by Woods on a Snowy Evening" by Robert Frost, played over and over in my mind:

The woods are lovely, dark and deep,
But I have promises to keep,
And miles to go before I sleep,
And miles to go before I sleep.

Our checkpoint for that night was Coalinga, California, and while I'm not exactly sure how it's supposed to be pronounced, I know I am still unable to attempt to say it without giggling.

But before we hit Cunnilingus, we had to conquer San Francisco. While our GPS was adamant that we cross the bay via the Richmond-San Rafael Bridge, thereby avoiding the clusterfuck that is downtown San Francisco, our collective sense of adventure would not allow for such pussyfooting. We ignored our pissed off navigator's repeated verbal warnings and headed straight for the Golden Gate.

It was dark, and so foggy that we could barely see the famous bridge's towers even when we were directly underneath them, but it was still worth the nearly two hours we ended up stuck in San Fran's financial district afterward to say we went over it. (For me, anyway. Angela was less enthused.)

Once we were finally through the cities, though, with the rain still pouring from the pitch black sky, the day began to feel excruciatingly long. When the excitement faded the anxiety of the trip's purpose started to set in, and I rode the last couple of hours in a state of perpetual panic that my emergency stash of Ativan couldn't reach. When we finally reached Coalinga and our hotel I took a quick shower, melted into the warm darkness of the covers, and slept.

Kimmy Dee

***

The next morning we slept in and had a leisurely breakfast before hitting the road, with only about 300 miles to go until Palm Springs, and no planned stops in between. The weather was a bit overcast, but for the first time since I landed in Portland four days earlier we weren't expecting to encounter any rain, and the landscape began to reflect the dryness.

I amazingly rode that entire leg of the trip without even the threat of a panic attack, and by early afternoon we were sur-rounded by mountains on both sides for the first time since leaving Oregon, as we traversed the San Gorgonio Pass toward Palm Springs.

Wind turbines stretched as far as the eye could see as we entered Coachella Valley, and once again I was struck by the gall of California. Seriously, who did these fucks think they were, harnessing all this natural energy? If God wanted us to power our cities with wind, he wouldn't have made dead dinosaurs so deliciously oily.

Upon our arrival in Palm Springs we had a much needed lunch and cocktail before checking into our home for the next three nights. At that point Angela had some work stuff to catch up on, so I set off on a solo walk. Our hotel was right on the main drag, and I was eager to explore, and to stretch my butt.

Palm Springs boasts a unique culture for such a small town… or at least it felt strange to my tiny Midwestern brain. Most of the people I encountered were either conservative old white people or flaming hot gay boys, and the tourism industry perfectly catered to both. The evangelical asshats of my home-town had led me to believe that these two societal factions could never coexist harmoniously, but Sonny Bono's little desert paradise blasts that antiquated myth into an exploding rainbow of fabulous Ronald Reagan-shaped confetti.

I figured I'd do a little window shopping, or perhaps find a café to park my easily exhausted butt at for a bit. The first

street I walked down was flanked by bars, and situated between one of the bars and an upscale boutique was a small card shop. I had tried to buy a small gift for my daughter from every leg of the journey, so I decided to step in to see if they had any knickknacks that my darling little princess might fancy.

The cards themselves were displayed in the entryway of the shop, and it didn't strike me as strange that most featured images of men in various stages of undress. You can't even peruse the "Her Birthday" section of a Hallmark store without being surrounded by shirtless cowboys and musclebound firemen; the more cliché the better when it comes to littering the planet with barely glanced at greeting cards. But as I thrust myself deeper and deeper into the cavernous store, one thing became abundantly clear: I was *not* going to find a gift for my seven-year-old girl here.

I'm not sure if it was the *21 flavors of lube* display or the hanging strands of anal beads that looked roughly the size of baseballs, but it soon became glaringly apparent that I wouldn't be finding anything for myself, either. And by glaringly, I mean the guy manning the register rocking skin tight shorty shorts and platform cowboy boots was shooting me a death stare so severe it made my vagina pucker. Or maybe that was the eye-level shelf display of gargantuan dildos, succinctly labeled '*Giant Black Cocks*.'

I tried to feign casual interest in the wares as I made my way back to the exit, as though I totally waltzed into the gay sex shop on purpose (Why, what do *you* do for fun on Tuesday afternoons?) but I don't think I came off as cool and collected as I was going for when I tripped over the sidewalk on my way out and was nearly run over by a shuttle van packed with senior citizens barreling toward the casino.

And, with that, I had officially arrived in Palm Springs.

Kimmy Dee

***

After my near-dildo experience I stuck strictly to the sidewalks, and soon I found myself strutting along the Palm Springs' Walk of Fame, which is where the truly influential celebrities achieve sidewalk star immortalization. Hollywood can keep its overly idolized sex symbols; Palm Springs will continue to laud the real contributors to the entertainment industry, such as Cheeta the Chimp, and the lady from that one Tide commercial that aired in 1986.

I headed back to the hotel and handed Angela her hair brush; I wanted to have one final drink before shifting my brain from vacation mode to emotional wreck. My dad's surviving siblings had arrived in town a few days ahead of us, and we were meeting them for dinner to finalize plans for the ash spreading to take place the following day.

My aunt and two uncles met us at our hotel, and after exchanging awkward niceties the five of us set out on foot to find a place to eat.

Not even a block from the hotel we encountered a quite inebriated young man facing the glass storefront of an art gallery that had closed for the evening, his hand pressed against the window, mumbling incoherently into the glass. He was shirtless, with fishnet stockings under his denim cutoffs and hooker boots. He seemed oblivious to the world outside of that darkened gallery, but perked up when my aunt suggested we have Mexican food for dinner.

"*Mexicans are extra-terrestrials mixed with Mongolians!*" he shouted at us.

I turned toward him and he pointed to a painting inside the gallery.

"This portrait is of me. Do you like it?"

The painting could very well have been of him. It depicted a fully nude man of similar build, seated in a high back chair in front of an elegant fireplace. A dog sat upright on what looked to be a bearskin rug, the dog's head effectively censoring the man's naughty bits. I nodded my approval, and my new street friend went back to mumbling desperately to the painting as my family and I picked up our pace, eager to put some distance between ourselves and the *Picture of Dorian Gay*.

We walked for about a thousand blocks before finally deciding to dine at the restaurant right next door to the fucking hotel, so I was already a bit irritated when I ordered water and the waiter asked if I'd like "local, bottled, or sparkling?" It was the most Southern California question I'd ever been asked, and I'm pretty sure getting uppity about water sources during a drought is the exact reason the rest of the country is secretly rooting for the whole damn state to crumble into the Pacific.

After fumbling with the question for far too long I finally traded my confusing water order in for a plain old organic, grass fed, free range margarita, and that decision was enough to improve my mood dramatically.

The food was amazing, and we sat and swapped stories about my dad and other relatives that had passed until the place completely cleared out, and all that remained were a couple of workers fluttering around, stacking chairs and spot cleaning random things, making it painfully obvious that they were waiting for us to get the fuck out so they could finally go home.

We eventually got the hint, and as we walked back to the hotel I noticed that my cheeks and stomach actually hurt from laughing so hard. I realized family is a funny thing; sometimes you spend so much time missing those that have gone that you forget to enjoy the ones that are left.

In the parking lot we set a time to meet up the following morning to do what we had come out to do, and my aunt and uncles piled into their rental car and headed back to their hotel. Angela and I returned to our room, where she once again put her hairbrush to good use, then tossed a folder onto my bed.

"It's your dad's writing," she said. "I thought you might want to read it."

She poured herself a glass of wine and settled into her own bed with her laptop, leaving me trembling as I thumbed through the pages. My dad hadn't been a writer; what she had found was a collection of papers he had written when he took some college courses in the early '90s, primarily labor law classes as he worked his way off the factory floor and up the union ranks.

Angela had read some but not all of them, and figured I'd appreciate how he managed to incorporate his smartass sense of humor into all of his work, regardless of the topic. The apple and the tree, and all that crap. Reading through an opinion piece about questioning authority, regardless of level, made me feel like I was hearing his voice again.

And then I came across a very short piece, only two pages long, titled "A Child's Heart".

It was two pages of raw emotion, a first person account of the guilt and anguish a father goes through when his marriage busts and he has to leave his kids behind.

It was something he and I had never talked about. I was six years old when my parents separated; I have very little memory of them even having been married. I went to my dad's on Sundays, I lived with my mom the rest of the week, and that was that. And in the nearly fifteen years' worth of Sundays I was able to spend with my dad after the divorce and before his passing, his feelings about walking away had never once come up. But then out of nowhere, on the day before the thirteenth anniversary of his death, the day before I'd return his remains to the Earth, I was hit with this:

The first Saturday night after the separation, Kimberly called me. She was crying. She said she couldn't sleep. I was to pick them up for the day on Sunday, and she was afraid I wouldn't show up. She was still crying when we finally hung up. She would never know, but so was I.

Angela had no idea the essay had even existed. The papers were old, and it was so small in comparison to the others that it was easy to miss. We both read through it a couple of times, and I noticed my stomach hurt again, but now it was from crying. I placed the papers back in the folder as carefully as if they were the Dead Sea Scrolls, and got myself ready for bed.

Despite being exhausted, I laid in bed reading for hours. I was too afraid to close my book and let my mind rest. I didn't want to think about tomorrow.

***

I woke up to the bed shaking.

I sat up and looked around the room. There was a steady, low pitched rumble, and as my socks hit the floor I could feel it in my feet.

It's the big one, I thought. *Just my fucking luck.*

A moment later Angela walked out of the bathroom, grabbed her comb, and went to work on her wet hair. I stared at her; she wasn't acknowledging the turbulence at all.

"Don't you feel that?" I asked.

"Yes," she said, and went back to her hair.

"Well, should we do something? Take cover, or whatever?" I was starting to panic. I had no idea what you were supposed to do during an earthquake. I had not prepared for this. I'm from Michigan, where the ground may be frozen but at least it holds the fuck still.

She looked at me like I had just farted out a hot air balloon, but then recognition crossed her face... and was followed by mad laughter.

Meanwhile the room was still shaking, and I wasn't sure whether I was supposed to crawl under a desk or stop, drop, and roll.

"I think we'll be okay," Angela said between giggles. "We're right above the laundry room."

I'll admit I was a little disappointed to learn my big California earthquake was really just a misaligned load of hotel linen, but I was thankful for something to laugh about over our morning coffee. Today we'd need all the laughs we could get. Because today was it; the culmination of our journey. A pilgrimage that had taken thirteen years.

We took a walk before we went to pick up the others. The sky was flawlessly blue, and I couldn't get enough of the contrast between it and the green fanning leaves of the palm trees with the desert mountains in the distance. A lot had changed in my life in thirteen years, but not here. And certainly not among the redwoods. I had come all this way to find peace within myself through nature, and nature was holding up its end of the bargain.

Now it was my turn.

We picked up my uncles and aunt, and headed to the place. *His* place. He had chosen it. It was outside of town, at a specific point along a certain hiking path, and it belonged to him and Angela. It was where he had proposed to her when his cancer was in remission. It was a place that would always represent happiness and hope, and it was where he belonged.

A picture of my dad in this place had been hanging in all of my various living rooms for the past thirteen years. Being there made me lightheaded. Starstruck, really. It was like being on the set of a beloved television show; everything looked so strange, yet so familiar. We spent an hour or so just poking around, not talking, just letting the energy of the place soak into our skin.

Eventually it became time to do what we had come there to do. My uncle said a few words. I reached into the plastic bag that held "Pat" – the body of my father, which I had last seen cold and lifeless thirteen years ago. I took a pinch of the gray sand and let it sprinkle down into the creek below. Everyone was still; the only noise was the slow trickle of the water as it snaked across the canyon.

Then, I poured.

Finding Pat

And pouring is all that it was. The "spreading" that is so romanticized is left to the wind and the water. I was crouched on a rock over a tiny creek; I had limited mobility to actually spread. And since it was a sunny, calm day in the canyon, and the creek flowed like the stagnant current of Rapunzel's shower drain, the ashes kind of just piled up around my feet like the world's saddest sand castle.

So instead of pondering the emotional significance of what I was doing, my brain zeroed in on this problem of physical science. As I poured the rest I tried to spread it around a little more, but to no avail. No one said anything, but who is going to tell someone they dumped out their dead dad wrong?

I couldn't accept that we came all this way just to leave him there as a sad lump of dirt, so I got down on my knees and pushed the pile with my hands into the water, letting it dilute and dissipate as the creek finally carried him away.

And, just like that, we were done.

I sat against a tree and watched the water for a long time. My family gave me space. And I began to think about what an accomplishment it had been for me to make this journey, when my rampant anxiety so often kept me from even leaving the house for something as simple as getting a bite to eat. And I wondered how different my life would have been if my dad, my rock, was still alive.

I poured out more than my dad's ashes that day. I unloaded many of the insecurities that were weighing me down. I let go of the excuses I had been clinging to for why I don't reach for what I want out of life. I dumped my hopelessness. But mostly it was ashes, because there really was a lot of dad sand in that fucking bag. I had always thought of cremation as reducing the body to a small fluffy pile of dust, ready to flutter away on the light breeze like an ethereal butterfly, but in reality you're left with about a ten pound brick of death dirt.

Eventually we gathered back together, and we decided to take a nice group picture before leaving the canyon. My aunt set up her camera's timer and we huddled together to say cheese. As the timer ticked down I whispered to my uncle

Jim to drop his pants and moon the camera. He needed no further urging, but he was a little slow on the drop and the picture turned out with him half turned around while seductively baring one ass cheek, while the other four of us smiled sweetly. And soon my cheeks hurt from laughing again, and it seemed that things might be okay after all.

And through the heat of the desert sun I could almost feel my dad's spirit smiling upon us. Closing my eyes, I could even see him: He stood tall and proud, smiling ear to ear, as he shook his head and muttered under his breath: "What a bunch of fucking morons."

Anti-Climax

I DON'T MASTURBATE. It's not because I don't want to, per se, I've just never figured out exactly how. I'm not a prude by any means; my vagina just shrivels into a desiccated shame cave whenever my hand gets near it. But I assure you, it's much kinder to others.

There was one time, though, that I did actually manage to get myself off.

I had gone to one of those stupid sex toy parties that girls always throw and the guy I was dating gave me some money to pick up massage oils, because he apparently had no idea what those parties were about. Since there were no oils to be had, I instead used his money to buy a giant vibrator. Because it wasn't my money, so fuck it.

This thing was huge, with rotating beads, built-in clit tickler, all the good stuff. It was a monstrosity of modern autoerotic engineering. It was so obnoxious that I absolutely had to have it. It made for a fun conversation piece. But impressing my friends with the sheer girth of my sinfulness was the extent of its usefulness. That is, until one night when the friend whose couch I was momentarily living on was out of town, and I began having an anxiety attack.

All I had at his house, all that I really owned at the time, were like three outfits and this fucking behemoth of a vibrator. In an effort to distract myself from my impending death, I broke out my B.O.B. (Battery Operated Boyfriend, which is how it was sold to me), and I came so hard and fast that I damn near died from that instead.

I realized then that what I had in my possession was a magical pussy wand, and it needed to be protected. I packed it away for safe keeping, only to be disturbed in case of an erogenous emergency.

So when the friend I was shacking up with became the boyfriend that knocked me up and we moved together into a tiny house, he stashed all of my precious (yet useless) keepsakes into the decrepit outdoor shed. As I got fatter and more horny I realized my precious Bob had been left out in the cold, but it was the dead of winter and there was too much snow to even get the shed door open, let alone dig my precious vibrator out of it.

When Spring finally arrived I was as excited to see my B.O.B. as I was to finally see the sun. I went to the shed, retrieved the one cardboard box with my name scribbled across it, ripped it open to liberate my libido's most beloved apparatus, and... MICE HAD FUCKING EATEN IT. All that was left of my one true love was some erratically dangling beads and leaking batteries. B.O.B. was dead, as were all of my dreams of self-fulfillment.

In an effort to make it up to me my boyfriend bought me a couple of new toys. But they weren't B.O.B.

He was all, "But I'll use them *on* you!"

Anti-Climax

And I was like, "Use them on *yourself*, Fuckstick!" And eventually they got packed away, never to be discussed again. But not in the shed. *Never* in the shed.

Eight years later I found myself nearing that dreaded mid-30s sexual prime, the mom years taking its toll on my fuckability. I was desperate for some sort of action, namely the kind you can get while watching Netflix alone and without waking the kid.

I tried feeling around down there, but not much was stirring.

I asked a group of girls I'm tight with on Facebook, "Hey, how the fuck you do masturbate, exactly?"

The overwhelming response was: "OMG YOU NEED A BUTTERFLY."

It sounded familiar. One of the bullshit toys my then-boyfriend-now-husband had bought for me was called The Butterfly.

So I dug that fucker out of the deepest depths of my closet. I shut and locked the doors to my bedroom. I pulled my pajama pants down around my knees, and pushed the button that brought that fluttery little bastard to life.

As instructed by my social media sex squad, I closed my eyes, took a deep breath, and began lightly teasing my no-no zone…

Nothing happened. Not even a flutter. It felt like a dentist's drill to a Novocain-numbed cheek; a nagging vibration that was best to not think about in great detail. But I had heard learning to masturbate took practice, and I'm nothing if not resilient. I held that goddamn thing there for a half an hour, and all I came away from it with was a nagging case of road rash covering the outlying areas of my cavernous gash.

The physical wounds may have healed, but the emotional trauma will last forever. Or at least until the next time I get properly fucked.

So, I can't masturbate. I also can't snap my fingers, cross my eyes, or overlook improper grammar on the internet. But to all of the self-satisfying naysayers out there that think I'm nothing but a wanker hater, I must say. . .

. . .what about B.O.B.?

ACKNOWLEDGMENTS

Heath Lowrance, whose incessant badgering forced me into finishing this book so he'd finally shut the fuck up;

Shane Lindemoen of Möbius Books, for believing in me and breathing new life into this silly little experiment;

My Family – for existing, and for occasionally leaving me the fuck alone to write;

All of my Friends that Live in the Internet – for never making me put on pants to feel pretty, and always pretending not to know me when we see each other in public;

And to my cats, who always make sure to remind me that I'm expendable.

But most of all, thank you to my readers. I couldn't do this without you, *both* of you, and I mean that from the bottom of my cold, dark, slightly-chafed vagina.

Xoxoxo

   –Kimmy

ABOUT THE AUTHOR

Kimmy lives in the Northern Midwest with her three beloved cats and one asshole dog. She also has a human family but they've asked to remain anonymous, for obvious reasons. They're pretty okay, though. Most of the time.

www.ingramcontent.com/pod-product-compliance
Lightning Source LLC
Chambersburg PA
CBHW050015090426
42734CB00021B/3282